IN THIS
Together

Secrets for Strengthening Your Marriage

JANIS LIPINSKI

Printed in the United States of America
First Printing 2021
First Edition 2021

ISBN: 978-0-578-30309-3

10 9 8 7 6 5 4 3 2 1

This book is dedicated to

Denny Lipinski, my beloved husband of 49 years.

Thank you for being my best friend,

an amazing husband, and a loving father to our children.

Thank you for encouraging me to pursue my dreams,

for supporting me through good times and bad,

and for loving me so faithfully.

REVIEWS

Whether you have been married for many years or one day, *In This Together* covers a multitude of situations and topics couples wrestle with. Like a good coach, Janis provides practical insight but also leaves room for critical thinking using powerful questions at the end of each chapter to discover how God might be speaking to you. The information and questions are artfully presented in a way that allows you to discover next steps the Holy Spirit is prompting you to take to strengthen your marriage.
Christy Gibas, Pittsburgh West Region Pastor, Crossroads Church

It is with joy and gladness that I recommend that husbands and wives read *In This Together: Secrets for Strengthening Your Marriage* by Janis Lipinski. Throughout the Bible, God encourages us "to be a Living Testimony." This means that our lives reflect our faithfulness to God and His Word. Janis and Denny **truly live** what they have learned from God about marriage and family. Their lives are genuinely a "Living Testimony!" So please read and put to practice what you learn in this book and become a Living Testimony yourselves!
Jennie Newbrough, Doctor of Ministry

Many of us likely enter into matrimony expecting the hearts and roses to last 'til death do us part but are shell shocked when real life sets in. Jan provides a road map to navigate the minor bumps but especially the hidden landmines along the way, with encouragement from God, the creator of love and marriage. She identifies common challenges in every season from newlyweds to empty nesters, sharing Biblical advice along with her own experiences from 49 years of marriage.
Susan Gross

Table of Contents

INTRODUCTION

Is your marriage exciting and invigorating or do you long for more? Do you feel cherished and loved by your spouse or do you feel neglected? Is it even possible to have a thriving, fulfilling marriage that lasts a lifetime?

In This Together, Discover Secrets for Strengthening Your Marriage shares God's wisdom for strengthening, protecting, and repairing your marriage relationship. The book imparts practical knowledge to help you better understand your spouse and how to communicate skillfully with sensitivity and thoughtful consideration to engage in more honest, constructive, and effective conversations that draw you closer together. I provide tips and strategies for encouraging deeper intimacy, and dealing with subjects like trust issues, infidelity, forgiveness, managing finances, raising children, blended families, and more.

The book includes introspective "Making It Personal" questions at the end of each chapter designed to help you identify the implications for your marriage and understand how to apply what you have learned to your own relationship. The questions are intended to be used for either individual, couples, or group study.

You and your spouse are in this together, and you both deserve the best life that your marriage can provide. Invest in your marriage and invest in each other to create the harmonious loving family you have always wanted. Don't settle for a lifeless marriage – be inspired to make the most of your marriage by committing to love each other passionately, completely devoted to one another as God intended.

I am not a marriage counselor, and you will not find any important letters after my name. If you picked up this book hoping to better understand your marriage from a psychological viewpoint and learn all about codependent relationships or clinical evaluations, you will be disappointed to find you wasted your time and money that could have been better spent on couple of Grande Frappuccinos from Starbucks.

I do, however, speak from experience, and after years of studying what God has to say about marriage and relationships, I have gained valuable insight into how to make your relationship vibrant, fulfilling, and long-lasting. I am a happily married woman who, due to trial and error, has discovered what works and what doesn't work when it comes to maintaining a happy, healthy relationship with one's spouse. One of the most foundational truths comes straight from the Bible.

> *"Anyone who listens to my teaching and follows it is wise, like a person who builds a house on solid rock." Matthew 7:24 (NLT)*

I have found that just as it says in the Bible, a wise person builds a house on solid rock, and a marriage built on the solid rock of godly Christian principles, definitely has a better chance of survival. Don't misunderstand, I am well aware that Christian marriages fail (33%) almost as often as non-Christian marriages (50%), but according to Glenn T. Stanton at Focus on the Family, a global Christian ministry dedicated to helping families thrive,

> *Many people who seriously practice a traditional religious faith – be it Christian or other – have a divorce rate markedly lower than the general population. The factor making the most difference is religious commitment and practice.*

> *The intuitive is true! Couples who regularly practice any combination of serious religious behaviors and attitudes – attend church nearly every week, read their Bibles and spiritual materials regularly; pray privately and together; generally take their faith seriously, living not as perfect disciples, but serious disciples – enjoy significantly lower divorce rates than mere church members, the general public and unbelievers.[1]*

I speak from my own personal experience, but God speaks from a place of infinite wisdom and irrefutable truth, so his principles are not something you want to ignore if you truly desire a rewarding, committed marriage relationship.

I have been married to the same man for 49 years. Were all of those years "over the moon" happy? Not a chance. In fact, while some years were better than others, a few of those years were downright miserable. In my weaker moments did I ever consider getting a divorce? Actually, yes. Every marriage goes through ups and downs, and sometimes it can seem more like a wild roller coaster ride where you are hanging on for dear life instead of smooth sailing on a blissfully calm sea. But in the end, if you hang on tight, let the wind blow through your hair, and embrace the peaks and valleys, the ride can be exhilarating.

I absolutely love to ride roller coasters. Any time we go to an amusement park, I quickly identify all the coaster rides and map out a plan so that I don't miss any. As I patiently stand in line waiting for my turn to jump on the ride, I look out over the track and see the places where the ride plunges down into the abyss or twirls around like a corkscrew, and sometimes I get a little surge of nervousness in the pit of my stomach, but I push past that knowing that I won't turn back now. I love the thrill of climbing the hill, hearing the clicking and clacking on the track, enjoying the suspense, just waiting for the moment when we start our descent. I hold my breath and then let out a shriek of sheer joy as the ride flies over the tracks, speeding down one hill and up the next, sometimes whirling in a corkscrew. It is such a rush as you feel your body surging with adrenaline. I totally love that feeling.

For some reason, my husband doesn't share my enthusiasm. We went on a long weekend up to Canada and I begged him to ride this roller coaster with me, Dragon Mountain, because you needed a partner or you couldn't ride. I usually make sure I have a riding buddy because my husband is not a fan, but this time it was just the two of us. After much pleading and promising him the moon, he reluctantly agreed to ride the Dragon with me. I think he was just tired of my begging. His plan was to close his eyes when we took off and not open them again until the car stopped. Personally, I can't understand that. I mean, how can you fully appreciate the ride, the suspense, and the excitement with your eyes closed? When we got off the ride, he was as pale as a ghost and visibly shaken. He didn't even look at me. The only thing he said was, "Please don't ever ask me to do that again."

Whether or not you are a fan of rollercoasters, marriage is almost always a crazy ride with unexpected dips and turns. One minute you are riding high enjoying the view, and the next minute you are plunged unexpectedly down into a deep dark place wondering how you got there. The basic relationship survival skill here is to be prepared and understand that life will bring challenges and difficulties that will throw you off balance at times, but God always makes a way for you to get through it. If you enlist the use of godly principles, make the effort to try to understand where your spouse is coming from, and make decisions designed to build up and strengthen your relationship, you will both find that the rewards are absolutely worth it.

At one point in your relationship, you made a solemn commitment to each other. You are a team, you chose to join your lives to each other, you are *in this together.* While I cannot promise you a blissful marriage from start to finish, I can promise that if you have a deep desire to make your relationship work, the principles in this book will give you some valuable tools and tips to help you make better decisions that will strengthen and enrich your relationship.

CHAPTER 1

FAIRY TALE INTERRUPTED

In the beginning, marriage is usually fun – romance and intimacy abound, and it can seem like you are surely destined for a fairy tale happy ending. The honeymoon was all that you hoped it would be and more. You are absolutely certain you made the right choice when you decided to marry the love of your life and look forward to every new day you get to spend with this magical person. Life is blissful, and it is meant to be.

God created the concept of marriage and designed it to be an enjoyable union of two people who love and support each other. In Genesis 2:18 it says,

> *Then the Lord God said, "It is not good that the man should be alone; I will make him a helper suitable for him."*

God recognized that man should not be alone. God designed us to be joined with another person, to have a helper, to have someone with whom we can share the joys and triumphs in life as well as the hard times. We are hardwired to function better together rather than being on our own. This type of relationship is meant to be a helping partnership, but also a loving pairing. In Song of Solomon 4:9, it speaks to a couple intoxicated with each other,

> *You have stolen my heart, my sister, my bride; you have stolen my heart with one glance of your eyes..."*

Love is a beautiful, a life-enriching joyful part of our human existence. When you find your soulmate, that person who rocks your world, you are both so eager to please each other because you are in love. And that love can grow deeper and deeper, richer, and more fulfilling than you can even imagine as the years go by, but first you will probably need to make a few adjustments. As you merge your lives together, you will begin to notice some areas of life where you are not exactly in tune with one another.

Sure, you may have noticed a few annoying habits. You know, those little things that bug you, but they seem so insignificant, easy to ignore. Life is good. And then it happens, the honeymoon phase starts to fade. Sometimes it happens after a few months or maybe only a few days, but inevitably, things begin to change, almost imperceptibly at first, but real life starts to happen. You begin to discover that your wants and desires may be just a tad different from his or hers.

♥ That minor irritation that kinda sorta bugged you before, magically seems so much more significant when he is late for dinner and doesn't bother to call. The dinner is getting ruined after all your hard work. Then you notice he left his socks from yesterday on the living room floor *again*. That annoying bad habit just went from insignificant to new ammunition.

♥ OR maybe you have great news to share and she doesn't return your call right away. In fact, she's been ghosting you all day. What's up with that! At first you were worried, but then you just get more and more angry. You can't believe that she couldn't find two minutes to make a simple phone call.

♥ OR maybe you want something from him like a little weekend getaway, and he is refusing to get onboard saying now isn't a good time to be away from the office. He says, "We just got back from our honeymoon three months ago, isn't that enough for a while?" You were hoping to recapture some of those magical honeymoon days, but he is always so obsessed with his work that he doesn't even notice that he spends less and less time with you.

♥ OR you have a bad day at work, and she is not as sympathetic as you think she should be. Doesn't she know how hard you work and how competitive your business is and what you are up against? You were hoping for so much more than, "I hear you, it's a tough world out there."

Maybe one or two of those scenarios resonate with you. I know I experienced all of them and much more. Understand this: You are two different people, and you cannot possibly be so naïve to think you are always and forever going to be on the same page. Marriage is definitely going to be a big adjustment, but it is worth the work it takes to keep it thriving. And make no mistake, it takes work.

So here you are, two previously very independent people who need to find a way to coexist in the same house. You come from two different family backgrounds, and every individual family has its own little culture, its own way of doing things. Not to mention that if you lived on your own prior to marriage, you have developed your own way of doing things. Add to that mix that men and women tend to think differently and approach things from a different perspective. Then there is the fact that as humans we are inherently selfish and want things our own way.

Wow! You may be thinking that sounds like a nearly impossible situation when you describe it that way. It is true that the adjustment can be an enormous challenge, but you can do it if you are willing to compromise and be flexible, but even more importantly, you need to be committed to staying together and willing to do the work to keep the relationship alive and thriving.

Of course, you will have differing opinions about what is the best course of action, the most considerate approach, the most expedient way to handle a problem, how to meet that challenge, or what to spend money on or not. This is absolutely normal and is to be expected. When this happens, not if, but when, you will need to know how to handle it without sacrificing the relationship. Yes, relationships are messy and frustrating, definitely challenging at times, but having a relationship that lasts a lifetime is beyond priceless. Let me share with you some of the adjustments we had to make as a couple early on.

We were married about a week, and we were thrilled to be married, but I was surprised how much of an adjustment it is to live with someone else, even when you are in love. We were pretty compatible with most things, but there were a lot of little things that he was accustomed to doing differently. One of them involved an alarm clock.

Most of your probably don't remember the Big Ben Alarm Clocks, but they were fairly popular in the 1970s. They kept good time, and they were very reliable because they were wind up clocks. If your power went out, your alarm clock would still go off at the appropriate time since it did not rely on electricity. This was *way* before the days of alarms on cell phones. When it was time to go back to work after the wedding, he got out his Big Ben and wound it up. My husband had to get up quite early for his job, so he had always used a Big Ben. I tried, I really tried to get used to his clock.

Noises really bother me, especially when I am trying to sleep. His clock would tick very loudly all night long. He would be sound asleep, and I would be lying there wide awake and all I could think about was TICK TOCK TICK TOCK TICK TOCK. It was driving me mad. I tried sleeping with a pillow over my head. I tried ear plugs. I tried putting the clock in the nightstand drawer hoping to dull the relentless noise. But I could still hear its incessant annoying TICK TOCK TICK TOCK TICK TOCK. As if that wasn't bad enough, when the alarm would go off in the morning, I was cruelly jolted awake by the shocking sound of the alarm blaring so loudly that I am sure it woke the neighbors as well.

I was cranky and exhausted. I finally had to deliver an ultimatum. I know that he relied on that clock to get him up on time without fail so that he would never be late for work, and I knew how important that was to him, but I simply couldn't take it anymore. I told him it's either me or the clock. After some debate, he chose me (yeah!) and he eventually agreed to put Big Ben in the next room. With Big Ben that far away, I was finally able to get some sleep. And believe me when I tell you, he could still hear it go off in the other room quite easily! That was one minor adjustment in the grand scheme of things. We successfully navigated that problem because we were willing to compromise, but other issues continued to come up.

The art of compromise is a fundamental building block for a successful relationship. Being able to talk it out and come to a workable solution is a key element in maintaining the peace, especially when things get difficult. Both parties need to be willing to give a little. This strengthens the bond between you, and it establishes a balance as you work together as a team to come up with a compromise.

Other differences we found were things like the toilet seat. Apparently, he never had to worry about putting the toilet seat down. He insisted on squeezing the toothpaste tube in the middle; everyone knows you are supposed to squeeze it on the end. I guess his mother always picked up his dirty socks because he seemed surprised that I was irritated by that. Another difference was that in his family, they refrigerated peanut butter and maple syrup and froze their butter.

We had one of our most memorable fights over butter. Yes, butter! I talked about this in my first book, but it provides some insight into making adjustments for the sake of your marriage. Our refrigerator broke, and it took several days until it could be fixed because the repairman needed to order parts. In the meantime, Denny took all our food from the refrigerator over to his brother's house and put it in his refrigerator and freezer for safekeeping. When I went to pick up the food after our refrigerator was up and running again, my sister-in-law helped me to load it into boxes. As I loaded the food from the freezer into the box, I saw that Denny had once again put my butter in the freezer. A surge of anger welled up inside of me.

It seems like such a silly thing to get upset about, but since Denny's mother always put her butter in the freezer, he took it upon himself to freeze my butter. My mother never froze butter, and I didn't know anyone else in the whole world who froze butter. Every time I went to use my butter, it was a frozen brick. I repeatedly told Denny that he didn't need to freeze butter. I showed him the package that said to "refrigerate" not freeze. But yet, he kept putting my butter in the freezer!

When I arrived back home with the food, Denny was waiting for me. I pulled the frozen butter out of the box and promptly threw it at him. Yes, I know, that was a little dramatic, but I was really frustrated. I shouted, "Imagine my surprise when once again I find my butter in the freezer! If you want to freeze butter, go home to your mother and freeze her butter, but leave my butter alone!" He didn't take that very well. He didn't say a word, he didn't have to – his expression said it all. He turned around, grabbed his coat and marched out the door. He took off in the car laying a strip of tire on the road as he peeled out.

At first, I felt justified. He just had to respect the fact that this was my kitchen, I did the cooking, and I didn't want frozen butter. I wanted to do things my way, and he had to stop comparing everything I did with what his mother had always done. To be honest, I was not that competent in the kitchen, especially compared to his mother. My culinary skills when we got married consisted of making toast and a ham sandwich. If it weren't for my Betty Crocker cookbook, we would have definitely starved to death. If it wasn't in that cookbook, we didn't eat it because that was all I knew how to make.

After three hours when he still didn't come home, I started to wonder if maybe I overreacted a bit. Throwing that hard frozen brick of butter probably left a bruise. Satan knows just how to use our feelings of inadequacy and jealousy against us. That's what this argument was really about – my jealousy of his mother because, in my eyes, Denny wanted to do things her way instead of my way. Don't we sometimes act really foolishly when we don't get our way? Even over silly things.

After four hours, I was pacing the floor wondering where he could possibly be. I was beginning to wonder if he was coming home at all. He finally pulled into the driveway five hours later at about 9:30 pm. He walked in and totally ignored me; he refused to look at me. I said, "I was beginning to wonder if you were coming home at all." With a straight face, he looked me in the eye and said, "I was busy freezing butter." We both started laughing. It really was a ridiculous fight. I apologized for throwing butter at him; he apologized for freezing the butter. All was forgiven. The best part of this story is that he never put my butter in the freezer ever again.

A sense of humor is like a pressure relief valve in an argument. It relieves the tension. If we can laugh at ourselves or laugh at a seemingly impossible situation, we can survive it. As a couple you will face many challenges, so don't take yourselves so seriously that you forget to find the humor in life. Billy Graham said,

> *A keen sense of humor helps us to overlook the unbecoming, understand the unconventional, tolerate the unpleasant, overcome the unexpected, and outlast the unbearable.*

When life gets tough, roll with it and keep your sense of humor. You will find that a sense of humor is vital to a relationship. If you can laugh at yourselves, you can get through almost anything. Some arguments can be ridiculous, some are more serious, but in the end, if you love and respect each other and are committed to making your relationship work, it will survive. You have heard the saying that "laughter is the best medicine." That actually originated in the Bible. Proverbs 17:22 says,

A cheerful heart is good medicine, but a crushed spirit dries up the bones.

If you can laugh together, have fun together, and enjoy each other's company, you will have "good medicine," but if not, you can look forward to a crushed spirit that dries up the bones!

Marriage often starts out like a fairy tale, and it is destined to evolve and change as you adjust and adapt to living with another person in the real world, but it is not destined to end in a nightmare. On the contrary, it is quite possible to have your happily ever after if you are brave enough to fight for your dream and committed to making it happen.

I believe that there are certain ingredients that are absolutely necessary to build a solid foundation for your marriage. Here are some must haves for a solid foundation:

♥ Respect – In the Bible women are told to respect their husbands, and men are told to love their wives (Ephesians 5.33). God made men and women different; we are wired differently, and God knows what motivates us. When women show respect to their husbands, it motivates him to love her; when men show love to their wives, it motivates her respect for him. This is essential to a healthy marriage.

♥ Trust – When your relationship is built on trust, it creates a safe, secure atmosphere that provides fertile ground for love to grow deeper and stronger. To build a trusting relationship, you must be faithful, honest and open, and a true friend desiring the best for each other. It takes time and effort to build trust, but it only takes a moment to destroy that hard-earned trust, so treat the trust you have been given as a sacred gift that is to be guarded at all costs.

- ♥ Love – It's not just about attraction based on sexual desire. It is so much more than that! According to the dictionary, love is strong affection based on admiration, devotion, and common interests; it is affection arising out of kinship or personal ties. You have these things with your spouse so nurture these things. Love is not just based on fickle emotions; love is a choice. You will experience many ups and downs in your relationship over the years. Sometimes you will feel "in love" and other times, not so much, but hang in there. As long as you work at staying united, I promise you that love will resurface. I have been married for 49 years, and I can tell you that hanging in there is worth it. Don't ever give up on each other. You can do this!

- ♥ The sturdiest of foundations are those built on the solid rock of Jesus Christ. It is not about just going to church as a family, but actually committing your lives to Jesus as Lord of your lives. Being obedient and surrendering your way to do things His way. The Bible itself gives us so many pointers on what love is and how to live it out, especially in 2 Corinthians 13, the love chapter you hear at weddings. I urge you to read this chapter for yourself and ask yourself if you would want a marriage based on these love principles. I would, and I do.

Love, trust, respect, and commitment are non-negotiable musts to have in a marriage, but the trick is maintaining that through the challenges and difficulties that life presents. Throughout this book I will be sharing valuable tools and tips that will help you to build up and strengthen your relationship with each other and with God, enrich your marriage, and prepare you to face the challenges head on. In the next chapter we will explore tool number one.

Chapter 1 Making It Personal

How did he (or she) propose?

1. Every marriage requires a period of adjustment as you get accustomed to sharing your lives with one another. What were some of your adjustments that you needed to make? What changes did your spouse need to make?

2. Every family unit has its own specific culture. How were your family cultures similar? How were they different? How have you blended those two cultures?

3. According to the dictionary, compromise is the settlement of differences by arbitration or by consent reached by mutual concessions. What type of compromises have you made to accommodate each other's needs?

4. Having disagreements is a part of every normal relationship. What was your first memorable fight about? How did you resolve it? Do you think it was resolved fairly?

5. *"A cheerful heart is good medicine."* Are you and your spouse able to maintain a sense of humor and able to laugh at your faults and failures together? Why or why not? If not, what can you do to integrate some fun and humor into your relationship?

6. Do you think you have all the necessary ingredients mentioned above for a solid foundation in your marriage? If not, how can you either build on your relationship to include these basic needs or how can you improve in these areas?

JANIS LIPINSKI

CHAPTER 2

THE WORDS WE SAY

The words we say play such a crucial role in our relationships. Communication is more than just words; it is an art, a skill to be developed. Learning how to communicate effectively and skillfully will help you in every area of your life – not just your relationship with your spouse, but in all your relationships. It is a skill that we use and practice every day, so it is well worth the effort to learn how to do it well.

What exactly is communication? According to the dictionary, communication is *the imparting or exchanging of information or news; the **successful** conveying or **sharing** of ideas and feelings*. Sounds easy, right? Unfortunately, there are many conversations that are not so successful and even fail miserably. How can that be avoided?

For a conversation to be productive and effective, there needs to be a back-and-forth discussion or **sharing** of information. If you want to be a good communicator, that is, have successful conversations in any relationship, you need two things: 1) to be a good listener, and 2) to impart information in a skillful, respectful manner to ensure that the other person understands and is actively engaged in the conversation.

The problem is that so many things can get in the way of effective communication. Let's go back to the definition and look at two key words: **successful sharing**. Sharing means talking *and listening*. In James 1:19, it says,

> *My dear brothers and sisters, take note of this: Everyone should be quick to listen, slow to speak and slow to become angry.*

This is excellent advice. If you are quick to hear, you learn what the other person is saying, thinking, and feeling, and you gain knowledge. If you are slow to speak, you can carefully consider your words to share in a way that is respectful, considerate, and effective. If you are slow to anger, the conversation is much more productive and beneficial. Once the shouting starts, the chance for successful conversation is usually lost, and you may both say things that you regret. So let's talk first about being quick to hear or good listening.

Be a Good Listener

Now you may think that listening is the easy part, and it can be, but there are skills that you can develop that will help you to become a better listener. Why do you need to develop listening skills? People who are good listeners are more popular, more productive, and better able to solve problems. They make better friends, spouses, and colleagues. If you are a good listener, people feel more comfortable communicating with you, more relaxed, and will naturally be more open to hearing what you have to say and more willing to cooperate with you. A good listener is typically perceived as respectful and confident and successful. They tend to build a certain rapport with others that generates feelings of trust.

Clearly, the benefits of being a good listener are many, so how do you develop those skills to become a better listener? Here are some suggestions:

Listen to Learn

The point of being engaged in a conversation as a good listener is to learn more about the other person. What is important to them? What are they thinking or feeling? What knowledge do they have to impart? How can you help them or collaborate with them? These are some things that you can learn that will help you to better understand people, their situation, their perspective, and their whys. You already know what you think, so listen to learn.

Have you ever been involved in a conversation when the listener seems to be only half listening because they are too busy formulating a rebuttal or anxiously waiting for you to stop talking so they can share their opinion? Or they make a comment that clues you in that they were not really paying attention at all. Are you ever guilty of this? This is a real conversation killer. In the book of Proverbs, verse 1:5 says,

> *Let the wise listen and add to their learning, and let the discerning get guidance—*

As I said before, if you listen attentively, you will learn something and better understand what the person is thinking and feeling; this will help to guide you in how to respond appropriately. Listening attentively reassures the speaker that you do care about what they have to say, you respect them enough to listen, and you value their thoughts and feelings. Proverbs 3:13-14 says,

> Blessed are those who find wisdom, those who gain understanding, for she (wisdom) is more profitable than silver and yields better returns than gold.

If you are the one doing all the talking, you are not gaining any wisdom. Listen to gain wisdom because it is more profitable than silver and more precious than gold!

Be Open-Minded

Being open-minded means to listen to someone else's opinion and be willing to consider new ideas or new possibilities even if they are different from your own or especially if they are different. Intently listening to someone else's viewpoint is a learning opportunity. It helps you to understand why they think the way they do.

Being open-minded and receptive to hearing new ideas without prejudice or judgment is generally considered to be a positive attribute. Being open-minded does not mean that you are agreeing with them or condoning their beliefs. It simply means that you are caring and respectful enough to hear them out. Don't be quick to rush to judgment, but rather show curiosity and ask about the reasoning behind their perspective. If you listen patiently to them, you will learn more, and they may be more inclined to listen to your viewpoint and your ideas.

Actively Listen

Have you ever talked to someone and they have that blank look that makes you wonder if anything you say is getting through to him? They may be listening, but they are not letting you know that they are listening, and that can be annoying. Chances are that they are not practicing *active listening*. What's that? Active listening requires looking the person in the eye and occasionally responding with an occasional nod or a short response like "I understand," "I know what you mean," "that's interesting," or "great!" Some type of response lets them know that you are engaged in the conversation and demonstrates that you are indeed listening and interested in what is being shared.

Avoid Distractions

We have all been guilty of being a bad listener at times. One of the most common culprits in these instances is distraction. There are so many things that vie for our attention to distract us. Sometimes we are distracted by the environment – a noisy child, a conversation at the next table, or noisy traffic. Or maybe you have something else on your mind that is claiming your attention. Or maybe your mind started to wander because you are bored. Or maybe you find it difficult to put down your cell phone or walk away from your computer, and you are only half listening while you keep checking the screen.

Obviously, this is not being a good listener and is offensive to the speaker. It is your job as the listener to let the speaker know that you are giving them your full attention. You can do this by actively listening, putting electronics aside, and maintaining eye contact. This will help you to stay on track with the conversation. Maintaining eye contact is important for both the listener and the speaker, and we will talk more about that later.

Don't Interrupt

People who interrupt a speaker are often viewed as rude, less friendly, and less intelligent. When you interrupt, the speaker does not have the opportunity to finish their thought and you may miss out on important information. When you interrupt, you are essentially telling the speaker that what you have to say is more important than what they are saying, and it changes the entire dynamic of the conversation as the interrupter tends to dominate the conversation. Be respectful and patient letting the speaker finish. You will get your turn.

The only time it is acceptable to interrupt is to ask for clarification. If you are unable to understand what the person is saying or not sure if you are understanding correctly, let them know so they have a chance to explain. It is better to ask for clarification than to jump to erroneous conclusions. Here you can phrase your need for clarification by saying something like, "If I am understanding you correctly, you are saying…" or "are you saying…?" Tell them in your own words what you believe they are saying and ask if you understood correctly.

To be a good listener, you must:

♥ *Listen to learn, listen actively by being responsive and engaged, keep an open mind, maintain eye contact, and don't interrupt.*

What is Your Body Saying?

Body language can sometimes speak louder than your words. In fact, some studies show that approximately 60% or more of communication is attributed to body language, so you need to be conscious of what your body is saying. Your eye contact, your facial expression, and your posture are all speaking to the other people in the conversation.

Eye Contact

One of the most important aspects of body language is eye contact. The benefits of maintaining eye contact in a conversation are many. Studies show that the person who sustains eye contact is generally perceived as more confident, more competent, and emotionally stable. They are considered warm, personable, more sincere, more trustworthy, and more likeable. Convinced yet that this is critically important to communication?

Maintaining eye contact shows respect for the speaker and tells them that what they have to say is important. It also suggests that you are tuned in and giving them your full attention, which brings a sense of intimacy to the conversation. This tends to create a connection or bonding that sets the tone for a more relaxed conversation that is conducive to greater levels of cooperation.

Another key benefit of good eye contact is that it often reveals more about the thoughts and feelings of the speaker. Eyes are often referred to as the "windows to the soul." The expression in someone's eyes can provide valuable clues as to what is really going on in their minds. Sometimes the mouth says one thing and the eyes say something completely different, so it is vital to pay attention.

Facial Expression

Facial expression is another key component of body language that speaks volumes. Thoughts and feelings show through on an individual's face. The lips alone can reveal so much. A smile can communicate happiness and positive energy, while a half smile or a smirk sends a whole different message. A smile that doesn't light up your eyes appears insincere or cold. Pursed or compressed lips can indicate anger or anxiety, while quivering lips hints at fear or sadness. Lips that are open or slightly parted imply that the person is comfortable and at ease, while a frown indicates displeasure or sadness. A furrowed brow could mean that you are concentrating, or it could be interpreted as a scowl. Whether you realize it or not, your facial expressions can reveal a significant amount of information about what you are thinking or feeling.

Posture

Posture is another indicator of your state of mind. Arms crossed suggests feeling vulnerable, defensive, or close-minded. Arms down at your sides infers that you are relaxed, comfortable, and ready to listen. Hands on the hips can mean that you are eager or could be a sign of aggression depending on what the rest of the body and eyes are saying.

If you are standing straight and leaning back you are more inclined to be disengaged or disinterested; whereas, when you lean into the conversation, you are perceived to be interested or excited. Proximity also matters. The closer you are, the more positive the conversation, but if you maintain a significant distance, you appear to be emotionally distant. If you are fidgeting, you look like you are impatient or bored.

If your communications are 60 percent body language and 40 percent the words you say, it makes sense that if you are not paying attention, if your eyes are on your phone or the dog next door, you are going to be missing out on more than half of what is being communicated. So be aware of your body language and that of the other participants in the conversation.

Assuming and Jumping to the Wrong Conclusion

When we first got married, communication didn't really seem to be a problem for us. He would come home from work, we would sit down to eat dinner, share our day, and the conversation flowed easily. However, as happens in every marriage that I have ever known or heard of, the fairy tale faded and real life entered into the relationship.

His work schedule picked up, and he was extremely busy. That left me trying to be superwoman, doing it all by myself. I felt really overloaded and really stressed. So what got left behind as a priority? Communication. It was the first casualty in our relationship. How did that impact our relationship? Definitely not good. We were like two strangers working side by side, barely interacting. This was a scenario that played out many times in our early years, especially after the children were born.

Denny worked in the road construction industry, so it was seasonal work. During the busiest part of the season, he worked long hours, and he would come home exhausted and hungry. I had worked all day too, came home and made dinner – the dinner that had to be reheated because he came home even later than expected. He was uncommunicative. Morosely staring into his plate, methodically lifting the fork and chewing.

I would get irritated because he's not saying anything. I ask him how his day went, and he barely grunts that it was long, and he would rather forget about it. Of course, I can clearly see that he isn't trying that hard to forget about it, or at least it looks that way to me. I put in a long difficult day too, the least he could do is talk to me. I needed someone to talk to about what happened at work, but when I start to tell him about it, he just says, "Can we talk about that later?" and proceeds to callously dismiss me by going in the other room, plopping on the sofa, and turning on the TV, leaving his dirty dishes on the table I might add! I go up to the bedroom and slam the door really loud to be sure he heard it.

Neither of us was being a good communicator. I assumed that he was ruminating over his day and ignoring me, just being rude, but the truth was more likely that he was just putting one forkful in front of another, just anxious to crash with no one demanding anything else of him because of sheer exhaustion.

In my first assumption, I am making it all about me instead of trying to see things from his perspective. He was obviously not thinking about or worried about my thoughts or feelings either. Here is a surprise: If you think your relationship will survive the "it's all about me" mindset, you will be terribly disappointed. As uncomfortable as it might be, you need to step into your spouse's shoes and take another look at your situation, reexamine the facts, and evaluate the results. It's amazing how much insight you can gain when you take the time to do this.

As you begin to see things differently, you may realize why your spouse is reacting the way he is. Use the insight you gain to be more understanding and cut each other a little slack. If you get angry and shut down, all communication is lost. But when you do make the effort to see from your spouse's perspective, it leads to better understanding and greater awareness of how you can be supportive of each other rather than at odds with one another.

Quality Communication is Critical

I know how busy and stressful life can be, and good communication is often one of the first things to disintegrate when you get irritated or stressed. It may seem at times that you just don't have time for "quality" communication. When you are in a hurry, your communication may sound gruff or demanding, and that doesn't always go over well with the recipient. Before you know it, tempers flare and you end up yelling at each other.

In retrospect, if you had just paid more attention to your tone of voice, or if you had just worded your request a little differently, or if you had just looked at the recipient instead of barking orders with your back turned, an argument may have been avoided. Quality communication may take more time and effort, but quality communication between couples is critical to keeping your relationship on stable ground.

In fact, lack of communication is cited as the #1 problem in troubled marriages. Making quality communication a priority is highly recommended! Make the time to talk about concerns you have and address the issues before they become a problem. You may not have the time or the money for date night and a sitter, but it is doable to take time out together even if it is just for a walk after dinner with a friend or family member holding down the fort for 30 minutes. If you only have a short time to spend together, make it count. Be intentional about your conversation. Keep it personal, but also keep it amicable. Remember, you are in this together. If responsibilities seem to be too one-sided, talk about it calmly, brainstorm and try to come up with solutions. Whatever you talk about, make it personal, keep it friendly, and make it count. Proverbs 16:24 says,

Gracious words are a honeycomb, sweet to the soul and healing to the bones.

Couldn't you both benefit from a little of that? I promise that it will be well worth the investment of your time and effort.

Focus on the Goal

So how do you communicate what you are feeling in a clear, concise way that is productive, effective, and loving? Quite simply, you keep your goal at the forefront. Your goal or your desire is to grow a lasting relationship built on love and mutual respect that is beneficial for both of you. You need to assume that this is what your partner wants as well. After all, you both made the choice to be together at some point, you chose each other, so build on that.

Tell him or her what your goal/desire is for the relationship and that you want it to be successful for the benefit of both of you. Explain what you are feeling. Maybe you are feeling that you are too often the one who is compromising instead of it being mutual. Maybe there is a particular incident that stands out as being unfair or one-sided.

Try not to be accusatory, but rather express how that incident or situation made you feel. Be truthful. Perhaps there was a time that your partner did compromise to meet your needs – remind them of that, thank them for it, and let them know how that made you feel loved and appreciated. A little bit of positive encouragement goes a long way.

Ask your partner if they want the same thing out of your relationship that you do and ask about their thoughts and feelings. Then you need to listen, really listen. If you are both working toward the same goal, have an honest discussion about what needs to happen for the goal to have the best chance of success. Listen without interrupting, without accusing, and without anger seeping through the discussion. Remember, good communication only happens when both parties share and listen attentively and respectfully.

What do you do if your partner doesn't want the same things as you do? What if the goals are different? You may just want to throw your hands up and say forget it, you tried but it didn't work out. My advice would be don't give up that easily. Relationships are hard work. They require persistence, consistency, determination, and prayer. We will talk more about prayer in a later chapter. As Nicholas Sparks wrote in Message in a Bottle, "Nothing that's worthwhile is ever easy. Remember that." I have said this before, and I will say it again – a loving, lasting relationship is worth fighting for with every fiber of your being. Don't give up without a fight! You are in this together.

Chapter 2 Making It Personal

What is the most memorable conversation blunder you have ever made?

1. Communication is defined as the successful conveying or sharing of ideas and feelings. We communicate with the people close to us every day. Do you think of communication as a necessary skill or as just something you do every day? Would you say that you are a skilled communicator, or could you use some improvement in that area?

2. In James 1:19, it says, "Know this, my beloved brothers: let every person be quick to hear, slow to speak, slow to anger." Typically, our first inclination is to be quick to speak and slow to hear. James is suggesting that we should reverse that approach. When you are in a discussion with others, do they think that you are *really listening* to what they have to say before you speak? How can you convey the impression that you sincerely care about what they want to share?

3. If you are quick to hear and slow to speak, what do you gain?

4. What are the four qualities of a good listener?

5. What are the three main components of body language?

6. Have you ever jumped to a wrong conclusion? What happened as a result?

7. Do you make quality communication a priority in your relationship? How do you do it? If not, how can you begin to focus on quality communication as a priority?

8. The goal of quality communication is to grow a lasting relationship built on love and mutual respect that is beneficial for both of you. What improvements can you make in your relationship to work toward that goal?

CHAPTER 3

FIGHT NICE

There is no doubt about it, you will fight because you are two people who have differences of opinion, differences in behaviors, and you probably have different goals and motives for what you do. Fighting can be exhausting and frustrating, but it can also be constructive and strengthen your relationship as you resolve some of your differences.

Fight nice sounds like a conundrum, but all married couples can fight in a way that is considerate and fair and productive. Fighting and resolving conflicts helps to provide balance for the relationship as you work through your expectations of each other. Setting healthy boundaries also provides balance as you both determine your personal needs, desires, and feelings.

When you have a problem or an issue that comes up, you need to talk about it. Denying or avoiding it never solves anything, and it can create a host of other problems. If you suppress your feelings, you run the risk of dealing with low self-esteem and suppressed anger that will eventually come out in other ways, like being irritable, short-tempered, and miserable. It is best to face a problem as soon as it comes up and deal with it before it turns into an even bigger problem.

You need to be open and honest about your feelings to keep those doors of communication open. Think of it as collaboration rather than a battle. In a collaboration, the goal is for both of you to come out as winners; in a battle, there is one loser and one winner, which, I hope, is not the desired outcome.

Remember, the end goal is to protect your relationship. You are in this together, so you need to work together and commit to communicating in a way that is respectful, loving, productive, and effective. So here are some tips and strategies for *positive* communication.

1. **Make sure timing is right.** Don't try to engage in a serious conversation when other person is cranky or tired or distracted or pressed for time. It is not a good time to talk about something important when busy preparing dinner or getting ready to leave for work or when the kids are listening, or when kids are noisy. Wait until you will have a few minutes of alone time and have his or her full attention and time for discussion. My husband would come home from work after a very long day tired, hungry, and tense. If I would wait for him at the door to dump all my frustrations and problems on him, it never turned out well. I don't advise doing it that way. After you have both had a chance to eat dinner and unwind a bit, ask him if the two of you can talk, or better yet, establish a time to talk. You might say, "After the kids go to bed tonight, could we talk about (the situation or problem). I'd really like to hear your ideas." Choose timing wisely.

2. **Give your spouse your full attention**, really listen, and maintain eye contact. This shows respect and a desire to communicate. Pay attention to body language. Don't try to multitask. That means no phone, TV, or computer. You may miss valuable clues in body language or tone of voice, and you may even miss some of what is being said if you are distracted. Again, make sure the timing is good. I am guilty of this, and it infuriates my husband. He starts to talk, and I will be listening, but looking at my phone. I have learned that the conversation goes so much smoother when I put the phone aside and focus my full attention on him.

3. **Do acknowledge that all emotions and feelings are valid,** especially those of your spouse. When sharing your feelings, be honest, but don't exaggerate. As soon as you exaggerate even a little bit, your listener automatically gets defensive and is less inclined to believe whatever else you have to say.

Don't use "you" or "always" language, like "you always do this to me."
First, "always" is probably an exaggeration of the truth, and that statement
is clearly an accusation that will immediately put the other person on the
defensive. Instead, use "I" language and be specific. "I felt really hurt and
angry when you didn't call to let me know you would be late." Your tone
of voice is very important too – rather than accusing, think of it as
explaining where you are coming from, trying to convey your perspective.

You can get your point across without being accusatory. It is tough to argue
against feelings. If someone tells you what they are feeling, respond with
acceptance and validate their feelings. You might say that you are sorry you
made him or her feel like that and perhaps explain why you acted the way
you did, providing insight into your thoughts and feelings. This allows the
other person to respond with an apology, and hopefully avoid future
misunderstandings or hurt feelings.

I learned this the hard way; we had more than one unproductive and loud
discussion until I learned to change the way I approached him with a need
or concern. Help each other to be better communicators by being
considerate of each other's feelings.

Rules of Engagement

To be an effective communicator, there are guidelines to follow that will
ensure that your conversations are productive and profitable. I have
mentioned some of these before, but they are worth repeating and
clarifying. I like to call this the rules of engagement, which is simply a list
of Dos and Don'ts for quality communication.

Let's start with the "DOs."

1. **Do be open-minded and empathetic.** Listen without
    jumping to judgement, listen until they are finished explaining.
    Try to consider what is being said with an impartial view. Also,
    try to look at the problem from his or her perspective. If you
    make the effort to step into your partner's shoes, it may give
    you some valuable insight that brings the two of you closer to
    compromising or finding a solution.

2. **Do try to understand** what is being said. If you are not sure, don't assume. Ask for clarification by paraphrasing what you think he or she means. For instance, "What I think you are saying is... Is that right?" This helps to avoid any misconceptions or wrong thinking. Jumping to the wrong conclusions can be a costly mistake, effectively shutting down productive conversation and possibly causing damage to your relationship.

3. **Do respond.** Whether it is just nodding or saying something to indicate you are actively listening – okay, I see what you mean, or hmm – just to let them know you are paying attention and in tune with what they are saying. Men often miss the importance of active listening, and most women equate no response with not listening or not caring. Pay attention and be responsive.

4. **Do give your partner a chance to express his or her feelings.** Show interest in hearing your partner's perspective. If you sense they are holding back, encourage them to speak. You don't want the conversation to be one-sided. You want to be fair and make sure that both of your perspectives have been openly discussed. You have a much better chance of maintaining a positive balance in your relationship and coming to a workable resolution if you both express your thoughts.

5. **Do pick your battles and choose wisely.** There are many things about our spouses that can irritate us, especially if we are really looking for something to fight about. Some of those small irritations are just not worth arguing over. If there is a significant issue that is truly causing you grief, then by all means, address that issue. But if it is just a minor irritant, be the bigger person (not the bitter person). Let it go, generously give some grace, and turn your focus instead to the things you love about your spouse.

Here are the DON'Ts:

1. **Don't interrupt**; wait until he or she is finished talking. Too often we assume what is coming next and jump in being defensive. Listen first, be patient and try to keep your body language under control (no rolling of the eyes or scowling facial expressions). You will get your turn.

2. **Don't be defensive or judgmental or critical.** Instead, try to be supportive and open-minded or be prepared to agree to disagree if necessary. Again, try to see the situation from his or her perspective and be willing to honestly consider how you would feel if the situation were reversed.

3. **Don't shout** or call each other names. Disrespect or forcefulness kills effective communication. If you have difficulty controlling your words or your anger, pray in advance for God to give you the self-control to guard your words. Psalm 141:3 is a good prayer to remember:

   Set a guard over my mouth, LORD; keep watch over the door of my lips.

   Use this prayer if you need some help to maintain your cool. But if you do see things getting out of hand and an argument starts to erupt, you need to take a break, give yourselves time to cool off and calm down first. Take a time out. That may take 15 minutes or an hour or longer, but no productive communication takes place when you are yelling at each other.

4. **Don't procrastinate.** Avoidance or denial doesn't solve the problem, it just prolongs the agony and can lead to feelings of resentment and suppressed anger. If there is a problem, deal with it before your little molehill turns into a huge mountain. Address the problem as soon as possible and actively look for solutions. The longer you let the problem fester, the harder it is to resolve amicably, so don't procrastinate.

5. **Don't stay angry**. In Ephesians 4:26-27, Paul warns,

> *In your anger do not sin: Do not let the sun go down while you are still angry, and do not give the devil a foothold.*

That is so true. If you go to bed with unresolved anger, you will probably not sleep well anyway. Your anger gives the devil a foot in the door to put a wedge between you. Many times, I would lay in bed fuming, thinking about all the things I would say to further express my rage, thinking about how I was right, and he was wrong, justifying my anger. The truth is that we were usually both wrong, and we needed to find a way to work through it or no one wins.

I've said this before, but bear with me one more time: Remember, you are in this together, so you need to work together and commit to communicating in a way that is respectful, loving, productive, and effective. *Communication is one of the most important components of a successful relationship.* Use good communication skills consistently to ensure that you are both understanding each other and united in your goals.

Chapter 3 Making It Personal

What is the silliest fight you ever had?

1. Fighting can be frustrating and exhausting, but what benefits can be derived from "fighting nice?"

2. Avoiding or denying a problem can have unwanted and unexpected consequences. Have you ever avoided talking about a problem for too long and have it backfire causing other problems?

3. Fights can seem like battles, especially when it is about something you feel very strongly about and you have differing opinions on the subject. When you argue, do you tend to see it as more of a battle or as a collaboration? What would it take for you to see it more from the perspective of a collaboration?

4. Proverbs 13:3 says, "Those who guard their lips preserve their lives, but those who speak rashly will come to ruin." These wise words advise us to choose our words with care so that we don't come to ruin. Using "you" and "always" language (you always do this to me) is much more accusatory and inflammatory than using "I" language (I felt so frustrated and angry when you forgot to pick up the kids after soccer). Can you think of examples of how to turn an inflammatory statement into an "I" statement?

    a. You always come home late for dinner. The least you could do is call.

    b. You never follow through when you say you are going to do something. You missed your daughter's game again!

    c. Where have you been? I have been waiting for you over two hours. How typical!

    d. You never want to go on vacation. You always make some lame excuse. I've had it!

5. What are the five "DOS" in fighting nice?

6. What are the five "DON'"TS" in fighting nice?

7. What strategies would be most helpful for you to incorporate into your communication skills?

CHAPTER 4

WHAT ARE YOU FEELING?

Every man, woman, and child on the planet has feelings and emotions they deal with every day. The dictionary describes emotions as *a conscious mental reaction (such as anger or fear) subjectively experienced as strong feeling usually directed toward a specific object and typically accompanied by physiological and behavioral changes in the body*. According to American psychologist Paul Eckma, we have six basic types of emotions: happiness, sadness, fear, anger, disgust, and surprise.[2]

Our emotions are significantly impacted by our environment, our life experiences, and our interactions with others, and they influence our behavioral responses. Our emotions are connected to other factors that shape our behavior, such as our mood, our disposition, our motivation, our personality, and our temperament. Some emotions are pleasant, and some are not. The unpleasant emotions we experience can stay with us, nag at us, drag us down, and become what is referred to as emotional baggage.

Emotional baggage can be detrimental to your emotional well-being if left unchecked or unresolved. It is defined by the Collins Dictionary as *the feelings you have about your past and the things that have happened to you, which often have a negative effect on your behavior and attitudes*.[3]

Everyone carries emotional baggage; it is normal, and it does have benefits. We can learn valuable lessons from our past experiences and carry those lessons forward in a positive sense. They can help us to manage future expectations, determine what we want or don't want in a relationship, and they can help you to cope with future challenges.

However, unhealthy emotional baggage accumulates when we go through some type of painful experience or unmet expectation, and we refuse to acknowledge or face the feelings they generate. Unresolved anger, guilt, shame, regret, trauma, or fear can weigh you down and inhibit your ability to be open to experience new things; thus, limiting your capacity to embrace life and live it to the fullest. We weren't designed to live a limited version of life. In John 10:10, Jesus says,

> *The thief comes only to steal and kill and destroy; I have come that they may have life and have it to the full.*

It is Satan (the thief) who tries to make sure your emotional baggage is weighing you down so that you can't experience the abundantly full life that Jesus has for you. Paul warns us in Galatians 5:1,

> *It is for freedom that Christ has set us free. Stand firm, then, and do not let yourselves be burdened again by a yoke of slavery.*

When you drag around unnecessary baggage, it can enslave you, hindering you from living in freedom, causing you to make decisions and choices that are jaded by past negative experiences. It not only causes you stress and robs you of joy, but when you are overloaded with emotional baggage, it can have an extremely negative impact on your relationships.

Certain feelings and emotions can be intense and difficult to handle, so we tuck them away to be handled later. Sometimes we let the problem stay in the "to be handled later" pile for a long time. The trouble with that is the longer we let the problem rest there, the more potential it has to get buried deep within us, and it becomes harder to recognize and more difficult to resolve.

Sometimes you don't even realize it's there you buried it so deep. Many years ago, a friend of mine had a situation where she was overwhelmed and overloaded for over a year. She reached out repeatedly and tried to enlist the aid of a specific person who would have been able to help relieve some of the pressure, and he did not step up. My friend was angry and frustrated with that person. Every time she would feel overwhelmed, her anger towards that person would flare and her hurt feelings would resurface; my friend was disappointed time and time again. Eventually the situation was resolved, and she thought that those feelings were resolved as well. Not so much.

My friend had stuffed that emotional baggage down so deep that she thought it was gone. What she didn't realize was that the disappointment and the anger was still there smoldering below the surface. It colored her emotional response to that person – she was impatient and easily irritated. She knew her reactions seemed unreasonable at times, but she didn't make the connection until many years later. My friend never told him how his lack of response wounded her deeply.

Because my friend never dealt with those emotions, it damaged their relationship. She denied those feelings. Her way of handling it was to suck it up and pretend to herself that the feelings didn't exist because she didn't want to feel that way. But she did. She was carrying emotional baggage and didn't realize it. When she finally realized years later she had repressed those feelings and what it was doing to their relationship, she confronted him, cleared the air, and forgave him. That person had no idea that my friend felt so deeply about it, and he sincerely apologized for not being there for his friend when he was needed. It is now a much healthier relationship.

When it comes to figuring out what to do about our feelings, we each tend to respond in various ways using various coping mechanisms, some of which can wreak havoc on our relationships like my friend's use of denial. Four of the most frequently used negative coping mechanisms include denial, withdrawal, anger, and substance abuse. Let's look at each one individually.

Denial

Denial is a common way of coping with a stressful situation or a problem. Instead of thinking of what to do and taking a proactive approach, the denier will purposely avoid thinking about the problem or situation and tends to engage in some type of distraction to push it to the back burner.

Denial could also mean that you are refusing to think that anything is wrong or refusing to acknowledge that you need help with something. Like when you have a persistent pain or ailment, and you resist going to the doctor. You may delude yourself into thinking that if you ignore it, the problem will go away. How often does that happen? Oftentimes, we are in denial about things that make us feel vulnerable or out of control.

This, unfortunately, is one of my problem coping strategies. I tend to be a bit of a perfectionist, which goes hand in hand (at least for me) with procrastination. I want to come up with the perfect plan, but I am not sure what to do, and I can't make a decision. Therefore, I refuse to think about it and do nothing.

Obviously, using this method, the problem is never resolved, and the little problem has the potential to develop into an even bigger problem if not dealt with sooner rather than later. This also increases my stress level because even though I try my best to not think about it, my mind goes there consistently (whether consciously or subconsciously), and I have to try harder and harder to push it away. The stress continues to build making me more irritable, short-tempered, and hungry for junk food. If you struggle with denial, try to be more mindful of your inclinations and instead of tucking it away in the "to be handled later" pile - pull it out, examine it, make a plan, and take action. We'll talk more about this later in the chapter.

Withdrawal

Withdrawal tends to happen when you feel so overwhelmed that you don't want to be around other people because engaging with others just takes too much energy. You may think that you are in no frame of mind (too sad or angry) to be with people who are expecting you to put on a happy face. You may be angry or irritated with your spouse, and don't want to engage in another argument so you withdraw by spending more time elsewhere. Men are good at this – they don't want to deal with something, so they go into their "cave" and don't come out until they are ready to either deal with it or forget about it. This method of coping can lead to feelings of isolation, extreme loneliness, and depression if left unchecked.

Even if you live in the same house, you may not be able to withdraw physically, but you can withdraw emotionally from your spouse causing a wedge to develop between you. The barriers go up, and the longer they are in place, the more difficult it is to tear them down.

If your relationship with your spouse is not what you hoped it would be, or you have had a painful experience (the loss of a loved one, a betrayal, a major letdown), the disappointment can be overwhelming and cause intense sadness. Depression is an insidious disorder that can be devastating to your physical health, your emotional health, and your relationships.

As soon as you think you may be heading in that direction, reach out to someone, whether it is a trusted friend, your spouse, or your primary care doctor, but get help. The sooner you identify this as a problem, the easier it is to deal with. Bonding and intimacy are essential for a positive relationship, and you can't have that with emotional distance between you. We were not created to be isolated and alone; we are better together.

Anger

We all get angry at times, but some people react to negative emotions or situations with anger as a coping mechanism that helps them to feel more in control. You may feel angry because of a wrong that was done to you, or you see an injustice, or are unable to control what is happening around you or to you. Justified anger can be positive if it gives us the incentive to take action to right a wrong, but unresolved anger can cause intense feelings that build up over time and increase stress or frustration. This type of anger can be unhealthy.

The thing about unresolved anger is that it can cause physical and emotional damage not just to you, but to anyone who is around you. Unresolved or "bottled-up" anger never really goes away. Rather, it festers and boils just below a thin surface with the potential to be unleashed on anyone within close proximity.

You need to learn how to accept what you can't control, take responsibility for your own actions, acknowledge that you cannot undo the past, and let it go. If you are angry with your spouse, talk about it. Explain your feelings. Why you are angry? How does that make you feel? What do you think needs to happen to resolve the problem? Are you being fair to each other? Have you tried putting yourself in your spouse's position? How are you willing to compromise to come to a better understanding? These questions may help you to communicate more effectively and respectfully to resolve your differences.

Substance Abuse

When we feel hurt or angry or confused or frustrated with life, we naturally tend to look for something to make us feel better, even if we know that it is only temporary. Your boss criticizes your performance, and you need to unwind by drinking a beer or two. You have an argument with your spouse that left you reeling, so you start surfing online for something to buy. Your back is killing you again, so you take a pill to help you relax and take the edge off. You find out your teenager has been skipping school and you reach for the box of cookies eating one after the other.

This is how addictions are born. We start out by just trying to make ourselves feel a little bit better by indulging in something that makes us feel good temporarily. If this becomes our go-to coping strategy, it becomes a regular habit, and we can end up battling an addiction.

An addiction can be to anything from alcohol or drugs to any other type of compulsive behavior such as pornography, sex, eating disorders, video gaming, exercise, shopping, gambling, social media, or even continual binging on TV. Some addictions are absolutely more harmful than others, but in the end, they intensify the problems you are facing and offer no resolution until you make the decision that you need to change your lifestyle.

Addiction not only takes a heavy toll on your relationships, but it can have serious consequences for your career and your health. A serious addiction will often take precedence over your responsibilities, your family, and your health wreaking havoc in its wake. If you suspect that you or your spouse is dealing with an addiction, there are countless organizations that can help for any type of addiction. Get help for yourself and encourage your spouse to get help as well.

Dealing with Negative Emotions

You are probably able to identify with at least one or more of these unhealthy coping strategies. I know I can. But the good news is there are also healthy coping strategies that can help to relieve stress, give you the confidence and the determination to face your challenges head on and deal with negative feelings in a positive way. I would suggest googling for a list of healthy coping strategies and choose one or more of them to help you cope with everyday stressors.

But you still have some of these negative emotions you are hanging onto, and you are hauling along this unhealthy emotional baggage. You need to lighten your load. How can you move forward and start the process of unloading? I have outlined several steps that will help you to face up to whatever is causing you a problem and deal with it effectively.

Identify the Problem

The first step is to stop distracting yourself and trying to make yourself feel better with short-term fixes or compulsive behaviors. Take a hard look at your past life experiences and consider what is causing you stress or anxiety. Identify the root cause. What kind of hang-ups are hiding beneath the surface? If you don't understand what is happening, you can't fix it.

For instance, if your boss criticized your performance at work, you were blindsided by the negative comments and you felt panic and fear that seemed to be out of proportion to the circumstances.

The root of the problem could be that you are concerned that it will have a negative impact on your livelihood and your financial stability. Look a little deeper. You may have experienced hunger or financial instability before, and it terrifies you.

You may be looking for a new job and are fearful of a poor reference. You may have experienced bullying or criticism that still stings and causes you to doubt yourself and have a lack of confidence. You never dealt with those negative feelings and you are suffering the consequences now.

Or it could be that your boss is the root of the problem because he is an unfair micromanager who is quick to unjustly criticize all his employees. It reminds you of your father – he was never satisfied with your performance no matter how hard you tried. Even though he is gone, you still carry those feelings of not being good enough.

Or it could be that you are not performing well in your job because a personal problem has been causing you to slack at work. You are burned out – you try so hard, but you just feel beaten down. What's the use in trying when no matter what you do you feel like a failure?

Whatever the problem is, you need to look deeper into **why** you are upset or worried or stressed. Ask God to reveal to you what is at the core of your emotions. Pray for insight and ask God for confirmation of what you think you are hearing. He will provide it.

Address the Problem

The second step is to evaluate what you discovered. Whatever the root cause may be, identify it and acknowledge that it is a problem that needs a solution. Examine your feelings and consider what may be holding you back from letting it go.

You may be in denial about the problem and hoped it would go away on its own. You may have just withdrawn from your spouse and friends basically licking your wounds in private. You may be angry about the situation and your lack of control and are taking it out on your family. You may have been indulging in unhealthy behaviors to distract yourself. Stop. Acknowledge the problem, make up your mind to do something about it, and commit to finding a solution. This leads us to step three.

Develop a Plan

How do you determine what action needs to be taken? My suggestion is to pray first. Ask God to guide you as you determine the steps you need to take to resolve the problem. Pay attention to any thoughts that pop into your head. Write them down. Explore the possibilities. Consider if these action steps are in line with Scripture and ask God for confirmation that this is the direction you are supposed to go.

If you are still unsure, share your thoughts and concerns with a trusted friend or your spouse. Identify several options, carefully evaluate each one, and consider the most likely outcome based on your choice. Decide on the best course of action and develop the action steps needed to move forward.

Take Action

Step four is simply putting that plan into action. You may have to adjust your plan and go to Plan B but that is OK. Be flexible, adaptable, and willing to compromise. You may need to develop Plan C or Plan D, but at least you are heading towards a solution. If you are struggling with the process or have difficulty figuring out what is causing your anxiety, I would strongly encourage you to seek professional help from a Christian counselor. A counselor can help you to better understand your feelings, how to cope more effectively in a positive way, and successfully manage your emotions.

Moving Forward

This process will help you to identify the emotional baggage, the hang-ups, the negative emotions, whatever is holding you back. Once you face up to what is going on, you can deal with it. Again, we can't fix what we don't understand. Once you develop a plan, you can take action towards a resolution. But to truly find release and freedom from what holds you back, enlist God's help in leaving it all behind you permanently.

We were not meant to live with negative emotions weighing us down and making us feel miserable. If you have unresolved feelings of guilt, shame, or regret dragging you down, God has a plan for relieving you of that burden. It is called forgiveness. 1 John 1:9 says,

> *But if we confess our sins to him, he is faithful and just and will forgive us our sins and purify us from all unrighteousness.*

We can't change the past or undo anything that has been done, but we can choose to leave it in the past where it belongs. We don't need to carry that emotional baggage around with us, because God loves us so much that if we confess our sin and ask for his forgiveness, he promises to forgive us and cleanse us of any sin. Psalm 103:12 (NLT) tells us,

> *He has removed our sins as far from us as the east is from the west.*

I'm not sure exactly how far away that is, but it sounds to me like our sins disappear completely once we are forgiven, and God doesn't hold them against us. By the same token, if you are harboring any anger, fear, or anxiety, they create a heavy load that drains your energy and vitality and keep you from living the abundant life you were meant to live. Matthew 11:28-30 says,

> *Come to me, all you who are weary and burdened, and I will give you rest. Take my yoke upon you and learn from me, for I am gentle and humble in heart, and you will find rest for your souls. For my yoke is easy and my burden is light.*

Bring your baggage to God, hand it over, and leave it! He will take care of it; he is willing and able. It sounds too simple, right? The truth is that simple; God can be trusted with your deepest darkest fears and pain. He is the healer of all our wounds, whether they are physical or emotional.

Seek God and Rely on His Guidance

Seek God through prayer and the reading of his Word, and you will find that this God-centered approach leaves you feeling refreshed, renewed, and greatly encouraged. Isaiah prophesized about the coming of Jesus and his mission here on earth. In Isaiah 61:1-3, he says,

> *The Spirit of the Sovereign Lord is on me,*
> *because the Lord has anointed me to proclaim good news to the poor.*
> *He has sent me to bind up the brokenhearted,*
> *to proclaim freedom for the captives and release from darkness for the prisoners,*
> *to proclaim the year of the Lord's favor and the day of vengeance of our God,*
> *to comfort all who mourn, and provide for those who grieve in Zion—*
> *to bestow on them a crown of beauty instead of ashes,*
> *the oil of joy instead of mourning,*
> *and a garment of praise instead of a spirit of despair.*
> *They will be called oaks of righteousness,*
> *a planting of the Lord for the display of his splendor.*

Jesus came to heal broken hearts. Even if your heart is shattered, Jesus can heal that deep-seated pain and transform your broken pieces and make them into something beautiful. Jesus came to set free those imprisoned by their sin, their fears, their addictions, those things that hold them back from being who they were meant to be.

Jesus came to give us a crown of beauty for ashes, to comfort those who mourn and replace their sadness with joy, to replace that spirit of despair with a song of praise. God is in the business of transforming lives that have experienced the oppression of pain, guilt, shame, or despair; he removes those heavy burdens and gives you rest for your soul.

It may take some time for you to feel a total release from those burdens; it is often a process. You may need to drop your baggage at the cross more than once because we tend to pick it back up every now and again. But if you let him, God will take care of any baggage you may have been carrying and replace it with a heart that is free and open to receive all that God has for you. You just need to be willing to let it go and hand it over to God. He is willing and able to take all your emotional baggage away, release you from the pain and suffering it caused, and set you free forever. All you have to do is ask.

One word of caution here, if you are still struggling with the process of dealing with difficult emotions or are having difficulty figuring out what is causing your anxiety or the root of your problem, I would strongly encourage you to seek professional help from a Christian counselor. A counselor can help you to better understand your feelings, how to cope more effectively in a positive way, and successfully manage your emotions. Praying, seeking God for direction and answers, and working with a counselor can put you on the right path for emotional and spiritual healing.

I personally have sought help from a Christian counselor at several times in my life, and I found it to be immensely beneficial because it provided the clarity, support, and encouragement I needed to move forward in a positive direction.

Chapter 4 Making It Personal

When you go on a trip, do you tend to over pack or under pack or bring just enough?

1. We all carry some emotional baggage – how much baggage do you carry? Will it fit in briefcase, a large suitcase, or do you lug around a trunk?

2. As children, we inevitably pick up some emotional baggage. If you experienced guilt, shame, fear, abuse, abandonment, betrayal, trauma, or extreme stress, you probably carry some emotional baggage. All of us have experienced some of these things. Can you identify some of the baggage you picked up as a child? Have you been able to unpack it and resolve it yet?

3. Four of the most frequently used negative coping mechanisms include denial, withdrawal, anger, and substance abuse or addictions. Which negative coping mechanisms do you tend to engage in? How has that worked out for you?

4. What would it look like or feel like if you let go of your emotional baggage? How would that improve you outlook and your quality of life?

5. Do you need to hand over some of your emotional baggage to God? If you want to hand it over, is there anything that is making you hesitant to do so? Take time right now to pray and ask God to take your baggage and experience the freedom that only God can give you.

6. Sometimes God instantly releases the burden from your shoulders, but sometimes it is a process that you must work through to truly leave it behind. What are some strategies that you can use to combat the unwelcome voice of negative self-talk that keeps wanting to drag you back down?

7. The Sword of the Spirit or the Word of God is the only offensive weapon we have been given to defend ourselves from the enemy of

our souls. The devil is well aware of our weaknesses and tries to exploit them regularly. What scripture verse can you use to defend yourself from the enemy? Memorize that verse and use it often.

CHAPTER 5

WHAT IF IT'S NOT THAT SIMPLE?

Embracing the Imperfections

We all have dreams for our future, picturing it to be healthy, happy, and successful with a loving spouse, happy gifted children, and someday grandchildren for us to spoil. The reality is that these dreams seldom happen just the way we planned, because life is messy. Sometimes problems beyond your control have a lasting impact on your life, and it appears there are no solutions to relieve your stress or the fix the problem situation. What do you do in that case? You do the only thing you can do – you plan according to the hand you are dealt.

You may have a spouse who is unwilling to work with you, unwilling to fight nice, or unwilling to learn more effective ways to communicate. That is okay. You can still do this. Even if one of you makes some changes to improve the relationship, it will have a positive impact on your marriage.

We can't control the way other people think or act or feel, but we can control how we think or act or feel. You can make positive changes in your responses and reactions that will be beneficial for both of you. If you make some positive changes, it may inspire your spouse to make some changes as well.

This probably won't come as a surprise, but if you are looking for the perfect mate, he or she does not exist. In fact, you are not the perfect mate, because you are not perfect either. We all have gifts, talents, and good qualities to share and bless others with, but we all have our faults as well. In Romans 3:10, Paul writes,

As it is written: There is no one righteous, not even one.

We are human, and no one is perfect. That is why it is so critically important to understand that in a relationship, there needs to be a healthy balance of give and take, and grace freely given. Grace is unmerited favor; in other words, you get a free pass at times even when you don't deserve it. So give each other the benefit of the doubt, be willing to forgive and forget – take the good with the bad.

What do you love about your spouse? Could that also be something you dislike about them? Take for instance the guy who is an extrovert – he is the life of the party, fun to be around, never a dull moment, funny, influential, popular, and spontaneous. However, on the flip side, an extrovert typically doesn't have as much control over his emotions, often relies on other people to make him happy, may be a risk-taker, and sometimes he just doesn't know when to shut up. Does that mean he's a bad person? No. It just means he is an extrovert.

One of the things I love about my husband is that he is so dependable; he's highly organized and very methodical. Is he spontaneous or adventurous? Heavens, no – he likes to plan everything. He always has a plan. On the other hand, I am more open to new ideas and enjoy changing things up; I am creative and adventurous, and I hate to be tied down to a plan. I would rather wing it.

The way our personalities line up, you might think that this relationship was doomed, but it works for us. We balance each other out. Does he get irritated when he asks me "what's for dinner?" and I say at 5:00 pm, "I'm not sure yet." That drives him crazy, but we never go hungry. I always manage to get dinner on the table, but I hate to plan – I like being flexible and often change my mind at the last minute. Not my husband. When he makes a decision, he sticks with it, and it totally irritates him when I spontaneously upset his plan. But he loves my flexibility and my adventurous spirit, and he admires my creativity. Even though we are direct opposites in some areas (they say opposites attract), we balance each other out.

My point is this: There will always be things about your spouse you wish were different, but you need to accept the person as is – flaws and all, just as he or she accepts you just as you are. In Romans 15:7, it says,

> *Accept one another, then, just as Christ accepted you, in order to bring praise to God.*

God is pleased when we accept each other, especially in our differences. We can all make changes and improve in some areas, but our basic personalities are what they are. Constantly trying to fight against something that is not likely to change is futile. You will be much happier if you learn to embrace your spouse's differences and imperfections and roll with it.

Traumatic Events

One of the things that can put a severe strain on a marriage is a life-changing traumatic event, something that threatens your dreams or your sense of security. It could be the death of a loved one, the loss of a job and financial stability, or a major health issue affecting you or a loved one. Maybe you were a victim of violence or are dealing with infidelity or a hurtful deception, a rebellious child or an addiction. Whatever the life altering trauma may be, it can have a serious negative impact on your relationship if you don't take steps to avoid it.

When life deals us a difficult blow, the most common tendency is to withdraw into ourselves for several reasons. This is happening to you, and you need time to process what you are thinking and feeling. You may be experiencing anxiety or fear or grief or all of those things. Depending on the situation, you may be feeling shame or guilt or anger. These emotions can be so intense that you feel raw and vulnerable, and this can make it hard to share with anyone else.

In a few days after the initial shock wears off, you will likely experience an emotional crash. You need to understand this is normal and give yourself time to adjust to your changed circumstances. As you ponder your situation, you may think that no one else understands what you are thinking or feeling. You feel alone in your struggle. You don't want to burden other people with what you are feeling, you would rather not be pitied, or you don't want anyone to see how defenseless you really feel. So you pull away and retreat into your own little world where the event keeps playing over and over in your head.

When my daughter was battling a rare medical condition, her doctor gave me news about the treatment plan he decided on and it shook me to my very core. I was blindsided, I kept thinking that this was a bad dream, this couldn't be happening. It would consume the next year or two of my life in a way that would be devastating for my whole family. For days, I was in misery, crying, angry with God, begging God for another way, lamenting the unfairness of it all. I was scared. I couldn't talk to anyone, not even my husband. Thoughts were swirling around in my head like a tornado filled with debris, not good thoughts.

I was struggling to make sense of what was happening. I was grieving for the loss of what I was expecting that was not to be. I felt so vulnerable, so helpless, so overwhelmed. After three or four days, I finally started to regain my footing a little bit at a time, but I was exhausted from all the crying and emotional turmoil. The initial shock had worn off, but I was still experiencing a whirlwind of emotions.

Life is messy. Unexpected things happen. Things that are beyond your control, things that scare you, things that knock you totally off balance and threaten your sense of security and stability. You will regain your balance. You will find a way to eventually move forward, but you need to allow yourself time to adjust. As difficult as it may seem, during this time, you need to try to maintain the necessities of life – good nutrition even though you don't feel hungry or just feel like eating junk, getting enough sleep even though it may be tough, and getting some physical exercise even if that is the last thing you feel like doing. You need to take care of youself physically. Allow yourself to be selfish and take the time you need to care for you.

If you are grieving a loss (loss of a job, a lifestyle, a loved one, or health) or coping with another type of tragedy, the best way to keep your marriage from falling apart is to make a commitment to each other that you will stick together. Lean on each other. You are stronger together.

Everyone grieves differently; men and women grieve differently. Just because your spouse is not showing the signs of grieving that you would expect does not mean that they are grieving any less. The five stages of grief (denial, anger, bargaining, depression, acceptance) happen differently for everyone as well. You may be stuck in the anger stage and your spouse has moved past that stage or may even bounce back into anger at a later time. The takeaway here is this: Give each other room to grieve however you need to, respect your differences, embrace your similarities, and give each other grace.

After the triggering event, you may find yourself unable to think about anything else. You try to distract yourself, but your mind keeps finding its way back to that thing you would rather avoid. You may experience nightmares or flashbacks. You may have suffered a blow to your self-image or have a more negative view of life in general and become untrusting of others. All these behaviors tend to shut others out, and you end up feeling even more alone and isolated.

Your spouse can be your lifeline. Lean on each other, spend time together, share your pain, share your thoughts and concerns, encourage each other to live, to breathe, to experience life. Focus on the positive things in your life, even if they are difficult to find right now. Be a safety net for each other and be aware of each other's state of mind. If you are concerned that your spouse may be slipping into a deep depression, encourage them to get help.

After my initial shock wore off, my husband and I were able to comfort and support each other. We had each other to lean on. I ultimately realized that even though this was not what I wanted, God would give us the grace to get through it, and he would sustain us through the next year or as long as it took.

As it turned out, the doctor changed his mind after talking with a colleague in another state (it was a very rare condition) and decided to go with a different approach that didn't have the same devastating impact as the original treatment plan. It was still challenging and difficult, but our trust in God and our support of each other helped to turn this scary event into a victory. We both had newfound confidence in the goodness and mercy of God. He taught us that trusting him would help us to get through any difficulties that life could throw at us.

Depression

It has been my experience that most of us go through seasons of depression during some point in our lives, especially when we experience a traumatic event. This is not abnormal or something to be feared; it is a normal part of life. But there is hope. David (referred to by God as a "man after God's own heart") experienced many traumatic events in his lifetime, and he struggled with depression at times. In Psalm 40:1-3, he says,

> *I waited patiently for the Lord; he turned to me and heard my cry.*
> *He lifted me out of the slimy pit, out of the mud and mire;*
> *he set my feet on a rock and gave me a firm place to stand.*
> *He put a new song in my mouth, a hymn of praise to our God.*
> *Many will see and fear the Lord and put their trust in him.*

We need to cry out to God, wait patiently, and he can lift us out of the slimy pit of depression. The Psalmist says that the Lord will set your feet on solid ground and give you a new song in your heart. Many will see that you trusted the Lord and give him the glory for his divine touch upon your life.

If you have ever experienced a severe depression, that's what it feels like – you are stuck in a slimy pit, like quicksand, and cannot pull yourself out no matter how desperately you want to or how hard you try. You need help; you need intervention. What better place to seek intervention than going to God for help?

God will definitely help if you sincerely seek him out, and I would highly recommend doing so, because he is the great healer of our physical and emotional bodies. But God also uses other people to come along side of us to help us overcome obstacles, and depression is one of those obstacles that can be extremely difficult to overcome all by yourself. You need the support and encouragement of others to help you to give you a boost to climb out of the pit.

The first, and probably the most difficult step, is to admit that you are struggling. To admit it first to yourself and then to others who can help.

Reach Out

Take that step of faith and reach out to others, preferably your spouse. This is the person who knows you best and cares about your personal wellbeing. If you are in a desolate place, it can be difficult to share your feelings, but you need to be willing to take the risk. Shutting out your spouse will only create more distance between you. I know you may feel like putting yourself out there and taking a risk sounds like the last thing you would want to do, but to get out of this rut, you need to take a leap of faith.

Reach out to your spouse, and honestly share your true feelings. It is not easy to be transparent and vulnerable, especially if you are afraid of what people think of you, even your spouse. You may not want to appear weak or defenseless, and your pride may make you resistant to opening up, but the only way to have a thriving relationship is through honest, transparent communication.

You may think that your spouse won't understand or that they may not want to hear what you have to say, but you need to take that first step and be real with each other. Acknowledge that there may be uncomfortable moments in the conversations; but getting over that hurdle will open the communication and allow you to take giant leaps forward in your relationship.

One of the other things that may be holding you back is your fear of being held accountable for making changes in your life. If something is wrong and there is something you know you should do to correct it, having someone to hold you to it is critical to moving forward. This gives you the incentive to make the change and stick to it. If there is an action step you need to take, tell someone so that they can provide the encouragement and support you need to make a change or take that first step.

As I said, your conversation may be messy, uncomfortable, or even hurtful. This is where you need to incorporate the skillful communication techniques discussed in the previous chapters. Be honest, transparent, respectful, and tactful. Be a good listener, actively listen with an open mind. Don't assume anything, ask questions. Go back and review Chapters 2 and 3 before your conversation if you need to.

If you want to deepen your relationship, you need to draw together, to lean on each other. The alternative is withdrawal and isolation which is unquestionably detrimental to the relationship. You may need to establish a new normal following a life-changing event, because some things will likely have to change in order to adapt, but it is worth the effort.

If you are finding it difficult to communicate effectively and productively with your spouse, reach out to a trusted friend or relative, maybe someone who has gone through a similar situation. It may help to seek out counseling, which is another valuable element that can provide long lasting benefits. Counseling can help you to decrease your anxiety or depressive symptoms. It can offer insight into your emotions and behaviors, and it can help to have a better understanding of your personal relationships and provide clarity.

Another option is to consider joining a peer support group, especially in situations involving violence, addiction, a major health diagnosis, or the death of a loved one. Support groups help you to recognize that you are not alone and give you an opportunity to express your feelings. You can also learn more about the challenges you face and gain insight into how to cope with your emotions and reduce stress. Support groups can be enjoyable and rewarding because you can build lasting friendships, have the chance to help others, and share a sense of hope.

These groups are usually very affordable or free. There are countless community groups out there. Reach out and give one a try. If you are unsure how to find a group, ask your physician, your counselor, or friends for input or simply do a Google search. Make a commitment to attend at least a few meetings. The first meeting may be slightly uncomfortable because it is new and strange; but go back for a couple more meetings to give it a decent chance of success.

Spiritual Support

As I mentioned before, life with our daughter was challenging at times. Our daughter was our third child. We had two healthy boys, and we had never experienced any major health concerns with either one. The most serious things we had to deal with up to this point were ear infections and stitches. When our daughter was born, she developed one medical problem after another. If we resolved one problem, another one would surface. By the time she was one year old, she had gone through five surgeries, and we were at the Children's Hospital of Pittsburgh more often than I could ever have imagined.

During this time, I felt so overwhelmed and so inadequate. I was constantly researching the latest diagnosis, trying to educate myself so that I could make informed decisions. There was no one I could talk with to ask for some guidance because her condition was so rare that the doctors were not even sure how to treat it. Her specialist consulted with his colleagues across the nation to decide on the best treatment plan.

Taking care of my daughter, consumed most of my time. My oldest son was 10, and he frequently took care of his 6-year-old brother while I cared for his sister. My husband worked long hours, so I often felt like I was doing it all on my own. My sister-in-law was a nurse, so she occasionally went with me to the doctor appointments to translate the medical jargon that I didn't understand, and I greatly appreciated her help. But for the most part, I was on my own. To say I was stressed would be putting it mildly – I was constantly on edge with no end in sight.

My world had changed dramatically. I lost contact with my friends because I just didn't have the time to socialize. My parents moved to Florida right before my daughter was born, so I didn't have them to lean on. My world was reduced to doctor and hospital visits, medical procedures and surgeries, physical therapy and home exercise programs. My mind was constantly focused on what I had to do next, making decisions about treatments, second guessing my decisions, and how was I going to get it all done. I was isolated, hyper-focused on medical stuff, and always fearful about what the future would hold.

The first three years were the most difficult. After that I suppose I adapted to our new normal and juggling ten things at once. In retrospect, I know I should have made more of an effort to reach out to people around me, but my pride kept me from doing that. I kept telling myself that this was my responsibility and I needed to tough it out. I didn't want to appear as inadequate as I felt. I made things so much harder for myself with that attitude.

My husband did his best to be supportive. He helped with the boys when he was not working, and listened when I needed to talk, but he was uncomfortable with "the medical stuff" and left all those decisions to me.

He would listen if I needed a sounding board, but in the end, the decisions were on my shoulders. Our relationship was stable because we kept the lines of communication open, but me personally, I was a wreck.

I know that the only thing that saved my sanity during that difficult time was my relationship with Jesus. I prayed fervently and frequently. I felt a strong connection with God since my early school years, but during those turbulent years, I grew stronger spiritually more than I had in all the years before. Jesus was my strength. He gave me courage and he filled my heart with peace even in the midst of the chaos.

You Are Never Alone

Just like my world was turned upside down with the birth of my daughter, you may be going through some life-changing difficulty. The world is full of challenges and disappointments, but you do not have to struggle through it on your own. When you invite Jesus to be a part of your life, you have a friend that sticks closer than a brother. If you let him, he will provide you with the support, the comfort, the guidance, and the confidence you need to face your challenges with courage and strength. God said in Hebrews 13:5b,

> *Never will I leave you; never will I forsake you.*

You are never truly alone if you allow Jesus to be in your life. Life is rarely all sunshine and roses; in fact, in John 16:33b, Jesus says,

> *In this world you will have trouble. But take heart! I have overcome the world.*

The bad news is that we know from our own experiences that nothing is ever perfect, things or people often don't live up to our expectations, and few things happen exactly according to our plans. The good news is that Jesus says to take heart, I have overcome the world. In other words, be encouraged because Jesus has conquered evil. In the end, the good guys win.

Purpose in Suffering

Those who stand with Jesus will experience the victory over sin and death, and most of the problems you have dealt with will one day seem less significant. While we will face difficulties, God has your back, and He is watching over you. The other good news is that our trials and tribulations we go through are not wasted, they serve an important purpose. James 1:2-4 says,

> *Consider it pure joy, my brothers and sisters whenever you face trials of many kinds, because you know that the testing of your faith produces perseverance. Let perseverance finish its work so that you may be mature and complete, not lacking anything.*

When we face challenges, problems, and difficult situations, we are growing in maturity, growing in strength, developing character and perseverance. Your suffering is not without benefit. During that time of pain or suffering, God is there to see you through it. He doesn't always "fix" it, but he will be right by your side to help you get through it. Deuteronomy 31:8 says,

> *The Lord himself goes before you and will be with you; he will never leave you nor forsake you. Do not be afraid; do not be discouraged.*

You will face trouble, but you will make it through with God's help. I thank God always for His presence in my life, especially since he has been with me supporting me and taking care of me without fail. He has provided peace in the midst of turmoil, strength when I needed it, wisdom when I have asked for it, and comfort at my most desperate of times. You may not be able to control the situation the way you would want to, but God has a plan and a purpose to use your circumstances for your benefit. In Romans 8:28, God says,

> *And we know that in all things God works for the good of those who love him, who have been called according to his purpose.*

So be encouraged. God has your best interests at heart. You will survive and perhaps even thrive through difficult situations when you trust Him. I remember at one point when I was particularly frustrated, feeling angry at God that my child had to suffer through all of this, I threw this verse back at him. I clearly remember yelling at God saying, "This verse is a lie, absolutely no good could ever come of this situation. It's just not fair that she has to suffer like this." Yes, I yelled at God. I cried out to him in a fit of anger at the injustice of it all. Thank the Lord, he didn't strike me with a lightning bolt. Instead, I heard this voice inside my head saying, "It's not over yet. Be patient. You will see."

I wasn't fully convinced then, but now I can look back and say that *YES*, that verse is true. All things did work out for the good for our daughter and me and the rest of our family. What we went through made us more resilient, stronger in our faith, more compassionate to others with health problems, and infinitely more grateful that we belong to Jesus, our mighty Savior, our Protector, and the Prince of Peace.

Remember before when I said that I was worried about what the future would hold? I worried a lot about my daughter's future. She was diagnosed with learning disabilities at an early age, and I feared that she would never do well in school, may never graduate or get a decent job; she may be dependent on us for the rest of her life.

My imagination was working overtime and I got on the "what-if" train. Big mistake. I eventually learned to take each day as it comes, do the best you can do, and it will work out. Maybe not the way you envisioned it working, but it will work out. But in my daughter's case, it worked out better than I could ever imagine.

Our daughter, in spite of the medical setbacks and the learning disabilities, did very well in school. In fact, she earned not only her bachelor's degree, but just a few years ago she earned her master's degree as well. She is gainfully employed with a terrific job that I know God provided just for her. Trust God to have your back. Ask him for clarity, for wisdom, for comfort, for peace, and he will provide.

Chapter 5 Making It Personal

We often have big dreams for our future as children. What was your "dream job" when you were 10 years' old?

1. We all have a vision of what we think our lives will be like – dreams for our career, our spouse, our children. Have you had one of your dreams completely fall apart and shatter? What happened? How did you overcome the disappointment?

2. What is the one thing you love the most about your spouse? What is the one thing you like the least, something that makes you crazy? Do these two things seem to be linked by a particular personality trait?

3. What traumatic event in your life impacted you the most? How did it change you? Are you able to see any benefits of having gone through that experience?

4. Have you or anyone close to you gone through a period of depression? How did you react? What were your thoughts? Was it difficult to understand? Was the situation resolved?

5. People tend to react to problems in one of four ways, they either 1) have the need to talk about it with the focus being on rehashing or reliving the problem, or 2) have the need to talk to others as a sounding board for finding a solution, or 3) clam up tighter than a drum replaying it in their mind over and over again, or 4) with total denial, refusing to think about it. Which category do you fit in, or do you typically have another type of reaction to dealing with a problem that's on your mind?

6. Matthew 6:34 warns us, "Therefore do not worry about tomorrow, for tomorrow will worry about itself. Each day has enough trouble of its own." We often waste time and energy worrying about so many things that never happen. Have you ever gotten caught up in the "What-If Train?" How did that work out for you?

7. What challenges have you faced that you think have made you a better person? How did you grow as a person either mentally, emotionally, or spiritually from the experience?

CHAPTER 6

ATTITUDE OF THE HEART

Honor One Another Above Yourself

In America, we are spoiled. We are rich compared to most other countries. The median income worldwide is roughly about $2,100 per year, which we can't even begin to comprehend. Most of us would struggle to live on that much per month, not a year. Because of our country's wealth, dare I say that a large percentage of our population have an "entitled" mindset. We want what everyone else has and think we should have access to it. At the very least, we expect to have a big screen TV and the latest cell phone and a computer for each family member. Hearing phrases like "you have to look out for #1," or "if I don't put me first, who will?" is not uncommon.

The "me first" philosophy is so prevalent in our society. If you put yourself at risk for other people some may even question your sanity. Think about it. We live in an era where people so are quick to defend their personal rights, often at the expense of other's rights. If you have any doubts about that, just look at the evening news or the postings on Social Media. The way of the world is "Me First!" But that is not God's way, and it is not the way it was meant to be. Putting the other person first in your relationship may sound risky at first or even absurd, but that is what you do when you love someone and truly care about them. Romans 12:10 says,

Be devoted to one another in love. Honor one another above yourselves."

This verse was addressed to all Christians in their relationships with one another, but it is even more critical in a marriage relationship. In our humanness, it is not natural to put others needs above our own, but according to psychological studies, it is honestly beneficial for you to do so. Hard to believe? Well, listen to the logic behind it.

People look for happiness in so many different places. Some think that if they just had more money, they would be happy; however, we have all heard the saying that "money doesn't buy happiness." Studies show that wealth indeed does not buy happiness; in fact, the wealthier you are, the more your happiness decreases, probably due to the stress of trying to hang on to what you have and always working for more. Achievements may bring satisfaction and happiness for a time, but it is short-lived. So where can we find happiness? What will fill that need? Compassion.

According to the dictionary, compassion is *a sympathetic consciousness of others' distress together with a desire to alleviate it.* Sympathetic consciousness, or in other words, caring about another person's happiness as if it were our own. If we are making a difference in our world by helping others, it makes us feel good about ourselves; it increases our level of happiness and leads to greater satisfaction in life. An attitude of compassion also has a positive influence on our interactions with others and improves how we treat ourselves. Compassion is one of the key ingredients of happiness.

Serving other people stimulates the pleasure center in our brains making us feel good and more energized. Volunteering is a reward within itself because it leads to increased feelings of happiness as we take steps towards alleviating a problem someone else is facing. It takes our focus off ourselves and our problems, and it redirects our focus to others, which in turn can reduce our stress levels.

Volunteering can also help us to see that others may have more difficult life situations than we do, making us more grateful for the blessings we enjoy. There have been countless studies done on the benefits of cultivating an attitude of gratitude.

When we focus on an being grateful, it puts us in a positive frame of mind, it has healing power for our physical bodies, and we feel happier and more fulfilled. Scientific studies have found that gratitude is associated with:

- ♥ Greater happiness

- ♥ More optimism/positive emotions

- ♥ New and lasting relationships

- ♥ Better health

- ♥ Progress toward personal goals

- ♥ Fewer aches and pains

- ♥ More alertness and determination

- ♥ Increased generosity and empathy

- ♥ Better sleep

- ♥ Improved self-esteem

Clearly, developing an attitude of gratitude is well worth the effort. There are difficulties and challenges that you face every day, but there are also hidden blessings that you have to search out or you could miss them completely. When we take the time to dig a little deeper, there are almost always blessings to be found. In addition, helping others is contagious because it promotes positive emotions and builds strong social connections which increases our general feeling of well-being.

Not only does having compassion, serving, and being filled with gratitude have lasting benefits that increase our happiness and make us feel good about ourselves, but it also pleases God. Paul says in Colossians 3:12,

> *Therefore, as God's chosen people, holy and dearly loved, clothe yourselves with compassion, kindness, humility, gentleness and patience.*

As God's dearly loved people, we are *commanded* to clothe ourselves with compassion, kindness, humility, gentleness, and patience. These virtues hold the key to fruitful, lasting relationships. Showing compassion, volunteering, and serving others is a win/win. If it has such a positive impact on your relationships with strangers, imagine the benefits of showing compassion towards your spouse and serving him or her! Another win/win, only the stakes are higher.

Serving Your Spouse

In a marital relationship, serving your spouse, putting his or her needs before your own is the only way marriage truly works. You married each other, committed to each other as partners for life. God designed marriage to be a loving, caring, reciprocating relationship where you meet each other's needs. We can't meet our own needs; that's why you sought out a partner. If you don't meet your spouse's needs, who will? It was intended to be you. If you don't meet your spouse's needs, there is a chance that the needs will be met elsewhere, and that can make your marriage vulnerable.

Your marriage is sacred ground and developing a Christ-like attitude towards your spouse is required for a healthy, thriving relationship. Jesus gave his life for us; he sacrificed it all for us. That is the model we should strive to emulate. In Ephesians 5:25 and 5:28, Paul says,

> *Husbands, love your wives, just as Christ loved the church and gave himself up for her.*

> *Husbands ought to love their wives as their own bodies. He who loves his wife loves himself.*

These are strong words that clearly state what God expects from husbands and how they are to treat their wives. The husband is to love his wife sacrificially, just as Christ loved us sacrificially when he gave himself up to be nailed to the cross. God even goes so far as to say that he who loves his wife loves himself. This is because a man and a woman are viewed in God's eyes as one flesh (Ephesians 5:31), so if the man is one with his wife and loves his wife, he is actually loving himself.

And by the same token, God gives clear direction to wives on how they should serve their husbands. In Ephesians 5:22-24, Paul says,

> *Wives, submit yourselves to your own husbands as you do to the Lord. For the husband is the head of the wife as Christ is the head of the church, his body, of which he is the Savior. Now as the church submits to Christ, so also wives should submit to their husbands in everything.*

Wow! This is not a popular point of view in our society where we fight for women's rights and fiercely seek after our quest to maintain our independence. So what does this mean exactly? The first time I read this, I thought that was then and this is now. Surely God doesn't expect women to just submit to their husbands in everything. But guess what – God is the same yesterday, today, and tomorrow. He doesn't change. Society has drastically changed, but God doesn't change. So how do we reconcile this with our current cultural views?

In my opinion, God has laid out the best plan for marriages to succeed, even though on some level it pains me as a woman to say this. Yes, a marriage relationship is meant to be a partnership where both parties are highly valued and respected, but there can only be one person in the equation who has the last say, and God gave that responsibility to the husband. Have you ever seen a company with two CEOs? Or a country with two Presidents? No. One person needs to ultimately be the one who says "yah" or "nah" in the partnership and make the deciding vote.

That doesn't mean that the man is always right or that the woman's input doesn't matter. It just means that ONE person needs to make the final decision. The husband is responsible for weighing all the facts and making the best decision he can. However, if he is wise, he will listen eagerly and respectfully to the input that his wife has to offer, just as the President seeks the advice of his cabinet as they weigh in on the decisions he makes. Proverbs 12:15 says,

The way of fools seems right to them, but the wise listen to advice.

If the husband is wise, he will readily listen to the contribution that his wife has to offer before making a judgement or decision. The bottom line, however, is that the husband is responsible for making the final decision, even if he is wrong. I know that for most women this is a difficult concept to embrace. Let's face it, when there is a difference of opinion, at least 50% of the time, the women are probably right. But be advised, it probably is not a great idea to say, "I told you so" when a decision he made proves to be the wrong one. Trust me, he will know if the decision was wrong even if he doesn't admit it.

So, let's get back to talking about serving. If your spouse tells you about a need that needs to be met, pay attention. View this as an opportunity to reaffirm the importance of your relationship and reassure your spouse of your love and commitment. You will both be blessed in return. When we serve others with a heart of love and gratitude, it brings joy to our hearts and God is pleased. In Ephesians 6:7, we are given a command.

Serve wholeheartedly, as if you were serving the Lord, not people.

We are to serve wholeheartedly, just like we would serve the Lord wholeheartedly. God is delighted when we serve enthusiastically, with a joyful heart, embracing the opportunities in front of us. Showing love and compassion to your spouse and seeing him or her through eyes of gratitude will not only drastically improve your relationship, but it will enrich it beyond measure.

This may be a totally new concept for you, and you may find that seeing your spouse from this perspective is not an easy task. It may even feel fake at first but putting your spouse's needs before your own is a choice. You can decide today that you will make every effort to serve your spouse with a joyful heart, and the benefits of this making this choice will be remarkable.

You can start with little things - anticipating a need and taking care of it before he asks, cleaning the snow off her car before you go to work, making a special dinner with his favorite foods, bringing her flowers for no reason, offering to pick up the kids, or completing that task that has been on your "to-do" list for a while. I think you will find that taking the initiative to please your spouse will not only make you feel good about yourself, but it will brighten your partner's day too. Once you get in the habit of serving your spouse, you may even find it addictive, especially if they reciprocate!

Let's talk about what to do if your spouse does not reciprocate, and you find that your needs are not being met. It can be very discouraging and cause resentment to build up. Ideally, both persons in the relationship should put the other above themselves. It should go both ways to be successful. So what do you do when you put your partner's needs above yours consistently, and they do not reciprocate?

First, you need to honestly evaluate your behaviors. Are you truly putting his or her needs above your own with love as the motivation or are you doing it from a self-righteous standpoint? Are you really always the one to bend and compromise or does your partner occasionally put you first too, maybe just not as often as you would like?

To be honest, relationships are often too one-sided, that is not at all unusual. This is another instance where quality communication comes in.

After you do a truthful self-evaluation, and if you are still thinking that you are always the one giving in and doing the serving, you have three choices.

1. You can either give up and forget about putting your partner first. You may think he or she doesn't deserve your efforts. Obviously not the best way to build a lasting relationship.

2. You can continue as you are going and hope that they "see the light" and suddenly begin to reciprocate, which may never happen and has the potential to make you resentful and bitter.

3. Or you can communicate your feelings in a loving way. Your communication must come from a perspective as a loving spouse who wants to make this relationship succeed. Remember, the goal is to build a good solid relationship that benefits both of you. Obviously, this is the best choice of the three to achieve your goal.

In all communication, remember the goal is to improve and enhance your relationship – you are in this together. Gently approach the subject with respect for your spouse's feelings and viewpoint. Be honest about what you are thinking and feeling and be specific about the issue at hand. Be positive by letting him or her know what you hope to see happen or change; offer encouragement by starting off with something currently being done right. You may even want to take partial responsibility for the problem if it is warranted. Offer to do your part to help accomplish the goal. Be flexible and willing to compromise to come to a workable solution.

Quality communication is a skill, an art, and consciously making a choice to use the techniques shared in this book will make conversations easier, more productive, and more effective. If things don't go well, don't get discouraged. If tempers flare, take a break and try again later. Apologize if you said something perceived as insensitive or disrespectful. Resist the urge to keep score (I did this and this for you and you did nothing for me) or bring up old hurts. Keep focused on the main subject of the conversation and on coming to a positive resolution. As you practice good communication skills, it becomes more natural and easier with each conversation.

Five Love Languages

Dr. Gary Chapman wrote a book called *The Five Love Languages* and it has sold millions of copies and has helped to improve millions of relationships over the last two decades. I highly recommend it. As it says in his book, "The premise is simple: different people with different personalities express love in different ways. Gary called these ways of expressing and receiving love the "Five Love Languages." They are Words of Affirmation, Acts of Service, Receiving Gifts, Quality Time, and Physical Touch. Each individual has at least one language that they prefer above the other... and this is where it gets interesting."[5]

Understanding your spouse's love language and fulfilling that need for love can boost your relationship to a whole new level. There is actually a quiz that you can take online to find out what your love language is. Just search "5 Love Languages" and click on the "Quizzes" tab. My love language is Words of Affirmation. I thrive on compliments, encouraging words, reassurances, and hearing "I love you!" This makes me feel loved, appreciated, self-assured, and confident in our relationship.

My husband's love language is Physical Touch. He feels loved when I cuddle up next to him on the sofa, when I hold his hand, when I touch his cheek, and when I spontaneously shower him with kisses. I could tell my husband that I love him, I could buy him gifts, I could spend quality time with him or do something special for him, but nothing says "I love you" to him like Physical Touch. That is what he needs to feel loved, and understanding that has helped our relationship grow and thrive. I would encourage you to find out what your love languages are and use that information to strengthen your relationship.

Chapter 6 Making It Personal

What was your first experience with volunteering?

1. Do you volunteer your time to any organization or cause? Why or why not? If you do, how does it make you feel when you give of your time? Do you believe that you are making a difference in the world?

2. Do you and your spouse openly communicate with each other about the needs you have and how your spouse can meet that need? Why or why not? If not, how could your relationship improve if you openly shared with one another?

3. Do you believe that you are doing a good job of meeting your spouse's needs or do you think that you need some improvement in that area? Do you believe your spouse is adequately meeting your needs? How could they improve?

4. According to Scripture, the man is commanded to love his wife sacrificially (putting her needs first) as Christ gave his life for the church, and a woman is commanded to submit to her husband as she would submit to Christ as her Lord. These are very strong directives to the husband and wife. Do you believe that you live out your marriage according to these principles or do you have a different arrangement that works better for you and your marriage?

5. They say that hindsight is 20/20 – if only we knew in advance how our decisions would work out! Have you ever made a decision that was contrary to what your spouse advised or suggested and it backfired? Did you hear "I told you so!" or was your spouse gracious enough to support you anyway?

6. What is one way that you can serve your spouse this week? What is one way that your spouse could serve you this week? Communicate with each other about your ideas for serving one another. It could be a fun experiment!

7. Can you guess what your love language is? What your spouse's love language is? Invest 10 minutes of your time to find out what you need to know by taking the quiz online.

CHAPTER 7

INTIMACY

When you hear the word intimacy in marriage, what comes to mind? Did you immediately think of a sexual relationship? While you can have a sexually intimate relationship, you can also have a sexual relationship without intimacy, even in marriage. The definition of intimacy according to the dictionary is a close, familiar, and usually affectionate or loving personal relationship with another person or group. A relationship that is truly intimate typically has certain characteristics – it is enjoyable, soul satisfying, fulfilling, comfortable, and thriving.

An intimate relationship typically grows over time as trust begins to develop and gradually strengthens so that both individuals feel safe with the other. There is a tendency to share personal information with each other, information that would not be shared with just anyone. As personal thoughts, feelings, and ideas are shared, one should feel confident that whatever is shared will be received with a spirit of genuine caring and concern for his or her wellbeing. They expect their secrets will be protected, held in confidence and not food for gossip.

Trust is the glue that holds a relationship together and it is the most vital component in the relationship. It takes a great deal of time and effort to build a trusting relationship, but it can be destroyed in the blink of an eye if one betrays the other. Guard your relationship closely and be wary of anything that could jeopardize that trust you have established. Without trust, the relationship will be on very shaky ground indeed.

Interdependence is another characteristic that is at the core of the relationship. You lean on each other, help each other out when needed, provide comfort and give selflessly of yourself for the sake of the other. You each respond to needs with understanding and provide support without a second thought, letting him or her know that they are loved. It is a reciprocal relationship.

Another desirable characteristic of intimacy is that the relationship is equal, not one-sided. Each partner shares, each partner is equally responsive to the other's needs. They think of each other in terms of "we" rather than seeing themselves as separate entities. There is a give and take that is healthily balanced so that each one feels equally loved and appreciated.

One more desirable characteristic of a healthy intimate relationship is mutual respect and acceptance without fear of judgement. It is a loving relationship where the individuals are tolerant of each other, willing to be empathetic, compassionate, and forgiving. (We will talk more about forgiving in Chapter 9.)

There will most likely be differences of opinions, arguments, and even fights that may result in hurt feelings or disappointment with each other, but as long as the trust is not broken, the hope of reconciliation is well within reach. You have each committed to the other, you have both benefited from the relationship, and you value the deep connection that has grown and strengthened. If both parties value the relationship and don't let pride keep them apart, they will find a way to come together through compromise and genuine caring for each other's wellbeing.

In a romantic relationship, it is always best to develop a strong friendship before the relationship becomes physical. If you have taken the time to build a relationship based on genuine caring and concern for each other's wellbeing, there is an additional protective layer that safeguards your hearts as trust is given a chance to grow and develop. The waiting may be sexually frustrating, but it makes the coming together in a physical relationship so much sweeter and satisfying because you first established trust.

I would be remiss if I did not share God's views on intimate sexual relations between a man and a woman. Hebrews 13:4 states:

> *Marriage should be honored by all, and the marriage bed kept pure, for God will judge the adulterer and all the sexually immoral.*

God's design for sexual intimacy between couples is intended to be within the confines of a marital relationship. That is definitely not a very popular concept in present day society, but I believe that it is designed this way for our protection. We often see people involved in sexual relationships too soon before any measure of friendship or trust is established, and it falls apart, leaving devastation and broken hearts in its wake.

Young people are especially susceptible to falling headlong into a lifestyle of casual sex that fails to provide what they are secretly longing for, what we all long for. As humans, we want to be wanted, to be loved, to be cherished, to feel like we matter. Casual sex, one-night stands, adulterous relationships, lustful relationships cheapen the beauty of what the intimate sexual relationship was designed to be. 1 Corinthians 6:18 warns us,

> *Flee from sexual immorality. All other sins a person commits are outside the body, but whoever sins sexually, sins against their own body.*

Why does God say "FLEE" from sexual immorality? Because he wants to ruin our fun? NO! Because He wants to protect us. He knows that a sexual relationship without love, commitment, and trust is unfulfilling and harmful, leaving us to feel empty and used when it doesn't work out. This life choice also comes with other potential risks and hazards – unwanted pregnancies, diseases, and emotional damage, not to mention the evils of perverted sex that preys on the weak and helpless with prostitution, child abuse, pornography, and sex trafficking. God doesn't just say "walk away" – He says FLEE. It is that crucial to your safety and well-being. Romantic sexual intimacy was designed to be a beautiful gift within the confines of marriage.

In a romantic intimate relationship, there is a craving of closeness, a strong desire to be with each other, and missing each other intensely when apart. There are usually frequent displays of affection. Too often, as couples are married for a time, those frequent displays of affection become fewer and farther between, and that is sad. As couples cope with maintaining jobs, running a household, raising children, caring for aging parents, and other responsibilities, the intimacy and close connection tends to take a back seat. Those hugs and kisses and cuddling sessions are so important to maintain the intimacy in a relationship. I'm not just talking about your sexual relationship. I am talking about that intimacy that makes you feel connected and intensifies that desire to share life together, a joining of the hearts.

One of my best friends unexpectedly lost her husband a few years ago, and it affected me deeply. It made me realize that my husband was "my person" – the one that I did life with, that I depended on, that I shared my deepest thoughts and fears and dreams with, the one who made my life rich and fulfilling. I realized that I had been taking him for granted, not ever thinking that what we have could be taken away suddenly without warning.

We now enjoy regular cuddling sessions, curled up on the sofa together, just appreciating being together and showing our love and commitment for each other by sharing those intimate moments. Those moments for me have become a special blessing, a time to express my gratitude to God for the gift of sharing my life with this man who is "my person." He is precious to me, and he will be loved forever and always in the deepest part of my soul.

You see, to be in a thriving healthy intimate relationship is more valuable and more precious than just a physically intimate relationship. Having that intimacy outside of the bedroom makes that physical part so much richer and more satisfying. Having that trust and confidence in your partner gives you all the more reason to pour your life into them, to give and receive love unconditionally.

An intimate relationship is a loving relationship. Whether it is with a close friend, a romantic partner, or a spouse, the guidelines for what love is and isn't is outlined perfectly in the Bible in 1 Corinthians 13:4-8, which is often read at wedding ceremonies:

> *Love is patient, love is kind. It does not envy, it does not boast, it is not proud. It does not dishonor others, it is not self-seeking, it is not easily angered, it keeps no record of wrongs. Love does not delight in evil but rejoices with the truth. It always protects, always trusts, always hopes, always perseveres. Love never fails.*

I don't want you miss this by just quickly reading that piece of scripture and moving on. Go back and read it again, but this time focusing on how you would feel if you were truly loved like this, according to these principles. Seriously, go back and read it again. How priceless to share a loving intimate relationship that lives up to this model! This is how God loves us! He models this for us by his gift to us. John 3:16 says,

> *For God so loved the world that he gave his one and only Son, that whoever believes in him shall not perish but have eternal life.*

He loves us sacrificially and unconditionally even when we don't deserve it. Romans 5:8 tells us,

> *But God demonstrates his own love for us in this: While we were still sinners, Christ died for us.*

Even if you don't acknowledge God, the gift of His son was freely given for you, and God continues to shower us with love and blessings every day even though we are not nearly as loving as He is. This is what I believe that we are to aspire to, loving others, especially those with whom we are sharing an intimate relationship, like God loves us. You may be thinking that it would be absolutely wonderful to be on the receiving end of this kind relationship, but to fulfill your part of the bargain here sounds unattainable. Remember that thriving intimate love relationships are meant to be reciprocal and interdependent; it must go both ways to work effectively. So how do you do it?

No one is perfect, so it would be impossible to always live up to this ideal, but this type of relationship is what we strive for, what we dream of, what we desire for ourselves, for our children, and those we love. Isn't it worth striving for? We have the capacity to love deeply, unconditionally, selflessly. Look at how we love our children. If you are a parent, most of you can relate to the fact that you would do anything for your child, even give your life for theirs if necessary. At least until they become teenagers, then it becomes a little more challenging. Just kidding. No really, just kidding.

Sexual Intimacy

A healthy sexual relationship is a vital part of a healthy marriage; it is like the oil that greases the engine to keep it running smoothly. Sex encourages connectedness; sex can heal and restore the vitality in your relationship. It is a gift from God, and it is meant to be one of the most fulfilling, enriching, and joyful parts of marriage. In Genesis 2:24, it says,

That is why a man leaves his father and mother and is united to his wife, and they become one flesh.

The man and woman are to become one flesh, joined together physically, creating a lasting bond that becomes even stronger than the bond between child and parent. Sex is a powerful force, and it can be phenomenally wonderful. But it can also become intensely complicated by many things – fatigue, unmet expectations, disappointment, conflict, past experiences, hurt feelings, anger – just to name a few.

When you first become one with your spouse, it may seem crazy to think that you will ever have a problem in the sex department, but as I mentioned before, the fairy tale is inevitably interrupted, real life happens, and things get complicated. How does it happen?

The enemy happens. Satan knows what a powerful driving force sex can be, and he uses it as the powerful tool it is to steal your joy, to cause trouble within your relationship, and drive a wedge between you. God created man and woman and marriage to be a beautiful foundation, to provide a base for a loving relationship to thrive. Satan, on the other hand, does not have the power to create anything, so he does the next best thing – he does all he can to distort and destroy that which God created.

Satan hates God, and he can't do anything to hurt God himself, so he goes after God's children as a way to hurt God. Satan will do anything he can to have his way. Don't you hurt when your children hurt? God loves us totally and unconditionally, so what better way to get at God than through his children. In 1 Peter 5:8, we are warned,

Be alert and of sober mind. Your enemy the devil prowls around like a roaring lion looking for someone to devour.

He wants to kill and devour you the same way as a lion kills and devours his prey. As if that is not convincing enough, in another verse in John 10:10a, we are told,

The thief (Satan) comes only to steal and kill and destroy.

Satan's agenda is to take all that God created to be beautiful and distort it, steal it, and destroy it. That includes your marriage, your relationship, and your happiness. What better way to destroy a family unit than working from the inside out? Yes, sex can be complicated by the enemy who seeks to destroy and devour, but God has created for us a way to rise above the nastiness that Satan has in store. You can fight against the enemy, fight for your marriage, fight for your happiness, and fight to enjoy a healthy, thriving sexually intimate relationship.

You don't have to resign yourself to settle for less, but unfortunately, many couples do. In fact, according to most statistics, about 75% of couples say that it is a struggle to maintain a healthy happy sex life. If you and your spouse struggle in this area, you are not alone. Is sex dividing you or uniting you as a couple? If you feel divided, you need to change your strategy.

Being divided on the issue of sexuality is divisive to your marriage. God acknowledges in the scripture below that a healthy sexual relationship where both the husband and wife are yielding to each other is the desirable outcome. This is clearly illustrated in 1 Corinthians 7:3-5, which says,

> *The husband should fulfill his marital duty to his wife, and likewise the wife to her husband. The wife does not have authority over her own body but yields it to her husband. In the same way, the husband does not have authority over his own body but yields it to his wife. Do not deprive each other except perhaps by mutual consent and for a time, so that you may devote yourselves to prayer. Then come together again so that Satan will not tempt you because of your lack of self-control.*

God recognizes that Satan, the enemy of your marriage, can and will use your desire for sexual intimacy to tempt you to go outside the marriage for fulfillment if you are not getting it from each other. Don't give Satan any opportunity to use your sexuality against you. The way you conquer your enemy is to fight him together. Your spouse is not your enemy. Give credit where credit is due. The real enemy here is Satan. You and your spouse are in this together; you are a team, and you need to come together to thwart your common enemy together.

One of the things you need to acknowledge is that maintaining a happy, healthy sex life is difficult. Expect it to be challenging, expect that you will be on a great path and then BAM! Out of nowhere comes a roadblock that rears its ugly head. The obstacle in your path is just that, an obstacle that needs to be overcome. It takes an intentional effort and determination from both of you to work towards finding a resolution.

There are so many things that can come between you in the bedroom. You may have resigned yourself to the situation as it is for so long that you may not even realize what the base of the problem is anymore. Do some self-evaluation to figure out what is happening. You may have some difficulty with this, but you need to understand what is wrong before you can fix it.

So how do you fix it? There will likely be several steps to go through to fully resolve the issues, but the first step (here it is again!) is communication – it is critical! It may be difficult or uncomfortable to discuss the issues that are problematic but talking about it is the first step towards resolving it. You need to be open and honest, willing to listen, and willing to work together to actively seek solutions. You need to talk to each other but talking to God first is wise – ask him for wisdom and guidance – then talk to your spouse.

Let's take a closer look at some of the areas where problems arise. This may help you to identify what you or your spouse may be struggling with. To have a healthy sexual relationship, you need to examine the four main elements that impact your sexual relationship:

- Emotional – Emotions play a huge role, and if you are not emotionally in tune with your spouse, if you do not have a satisfyingly intimate relationship outside of the bedroom, there are likely to be problems inside the bedroom. We talked about the value of establishing a bond of intimacy, that connectedness and affection that reinforces your commitment to each other. Are your emotional needs being met? Are you feeling hurt or angry and allowing it to affect your feelings toward your sexual relationship? Do you feel like instead of making love you are just having sex leaving you to feel used? These questions may help you to identify any emotional concerns.

- Spiritual – Sex is a natural part of life, and in its purest form it is freely giving and receiving, an act of pleasure through giving with an attitude of patience, affection, and sensitivity, feeling both passion and compassion for your spouse, causing you to feel at peace within your very soul. Past negative experiences or misconceptions about what God expects of you can hinder you, causing inhibitions to creep in and distort something that was meant to be beautiful. Talk with your spouse or clergyman or a Christian counselor to gain more insight into your thoughts if you have doubts or concerns.

- Physical – Physical issues or limitations can cause problems as well, especially with aging. If you are experiencing pain or discomfort, it naturally reduces physical desire. Feeling inadequate or having a lack of desire due to physical ailments or hormone imbalance is not uncommon. If you have concerns in this area, it is not likely to go away on its own. Communicate with your doctor to resolve the issues.

- Mental – There is a strong link between your mental health and your feelings toward your sexuality. Problems with depression, anxiety, stress, PTSD, or any other type of mental health diagnosis can have a significantly negative impact on your sexuality. Some medications used to treat these conditions have side effects that can lower your sex drive. Talk with a Christian counselor to get some assistance with brainstorming options and finding a solution.

Each of the elements of the sexual relationship – emotional, spiritual, physical, and mental – need to be in a state of healthy functioning to maintain a healthy sexual relationship. As I said before, there are so many things that can create barriers, problems that rise up between you and your spouse. It is difficult and challenging to maintain the ideal sexual relationship, but it is worth the work and effort you put into it because your happiness and the health of your marriage depend upon it.

No matter how awkward or difficult those uncomfortable conversations can be, you need to communicate with your spouse, your doctor, Christian counselor, or a mental health professional to resolve your problems as soon as possible. The longer you put it off, the more difficult it becomes. If you think you need help, don't hesitate – ask for it.

Remember, you are in this together. Don't blame each other; your spouse is not the enemy. Instead, work together as a team with a common goal at the center of your focus. I would also strongly suggest that you and your spouse pray for healing of your sexual intimacy. God cares about everything that you care about, everything that affects your happiness, and He desires for you and your spouse to enjoy a blissful and fulfilling sexual intimacy – that is His design for your marriage. Don't settle for less, enjoy life to the fullest!

Chapter 7 Making It Personal

Describe your first kiss.

1. What do you consider to be the most important characteristics of a healthy intimate relationship?

2. The author referred to trust as the glue that holds the relationship together. Do you agree with this statement? Why or why not?

3. What are some of the negative consequences of people engaging in casual sex that you have seen or experienced? How has that impacted your view of sex in our society?

4. Women feel more loved and appreciated when they are shown affection outside of the bedroom. Do you agree? Why or why not? On a scale of 1-10 (poor – excellent) how would you rate your spouse's satisfaction in this area? Would he or she agree?

5. Most men need to feel love and respected by their spouse. Do you agree? Why or why not? On a scale of 1-10 (poor – excellent) how would you rate your spouse's satisfaction in this area? Would he or she agree?

6. Satan is the enemy, not your spouse. He seeks to destroy your relationship, and he is the one you need to fight against, not each other. Have you seen evidence of this in your marriage where Satan drove a wedge between you? How did you resolve it? If you didn't resolve it yet, how could you begin to do so?

7. What are the four elements of the sexual relationship? Which area are you strongest in? Which area do you think you could improve?

8. Good communication is critical in this area. Is it difficult to talk with your spouse or others about sexual matters? What could make it easier for you?

CHAPTER 8

INFIDELITY

Infidelity causes severe emotional distress, especially for the one who was betrayed. Infidelity, according to the dictionary is defined as having a romantic or sexual relationship with someone other than the husband, wife, or partner or unfaithfulness. Infidelity can be one of the most devastating events in life you can ever experience. God warned his people in the Ten Commandments (Exodus 20:14) not to commit adultery, and Jesus distinctly states more than once in the Bible,

You shall not commit adultery.

In the Book of Proverbs in verse 6:32, Solomon states,

But a man who commits adultery has no sense; whoever does so destroys himself.

There is no doubt that adultery is destructive and sometimes fatally wounding to a marriage. However, infidelity may be viewed differently by those in the marital relationship. What does cheating or infidelity mean to you? Is it an actual sexual relationship, or is it broader than that? Some would include in emotional involvement or excessive flirting as infidelity, or an intense online relationship, or pornography. Jesus said in Matthew 5:28,

But I tell you that anyone who looks at a woman lustfully has already committed adultery with her in his heart.

In light of that passage, Jesus has a much stricter viewpoint on what constitutes adultery. If you view pornography as a betrayal, your spouse should be aware of your feelings. If you think that an online relationship is harmless, does your spouse feel the same way? It is important to talk with your spouse about exactly what your expectations are for your relationship so there is no room for confusion or misunderstanding.

According to most statistics, about 25% of relationships experience infidelity at some point in their marriage, and about 25% of those marriages end in divorce. Are you surprised by those statistics? I know I was. I was surprised at the high number of marriages experiencing infidelity, and just as surprised that 75% of those marriages, the majority, survived in spite of the infidelity. But some experts think that there is no way to really know the true statistics.

Why Do Spouses Cheat?

The number one reason why people cheat is because they believe that their needs are not being met by their spouse. The most common cause stated is a lack of intimacy, this could either be physical or emotional intimacy that is lacking, and feelings of neglect. The unfaithful spouse may be searching for a stronger emotional connection or attention that makes them feel more attractive or flattery to boost their self-esteem.

Men and women may seek sex outside of their marriage because of a desire for a more exciting, seductive sexual intimacy, feeling seductive, or hypersexuality, which is exhibiting unusual or excessive concern with or indulgence in sexual activity or an addiction to sex. There are times when the man or women claims to be happy in their marriage and still becomes involved in an extramarital affair.

Lack of communication is also cited as a leading cause for infidelity. I know I have said this before, but quality communication is so critical for a solid relationship. If you and your spouse don't know how to communicate well, there are bound to be issues involving frequent misunderstandings, erroneous assumptions, hurt feelings and emotional upset, and possibly deceit because you are not inclined to share your thoughts, feelings, and actions with your spouse. Once you start hiding things from your spouse and dishonesty creeps into a relationship, trust is compromised leading to other deep-seated problems. Poor communication, yelling or verbal abuse may be part of the problem as well.

One couple I knew professed to love each other deeply; they dated for two years before they got married. She thought she knew him well, but he was verbally abusive. It started out as occasional little digs, but as time went on, it became more frequent and more antagonistic. He would appear to be affectionate and loving one moment, and the next he would be saying hurtful disparaging remarks to his wife, belittling her not only when they were alone, but also in front of friends and family. This behavior resulted in feelings of low self-esteem and shame for his wife. Their marriage did not last long; it was doomed to failure. Hurtful words we say can cause deep wounds and can destroy a relationship beyond repair. A spouse needs to feel wanted, appreciated, loved, and respected. When this need is not met, the temptation to get those needs met elsewhere can become overwhelming.

When the marriage relationship is on rocky ground, there are so many things that can go wrong leading to infidelity. Unresolved anger with a spouse may drive a wedge between a husband and wife causing one of them to lash out, cheating for revenge against their partner. Or one of them may just want out of the relationship because they have grown apart or fallen out of love, or perhaps they simply want to move on for other selfish reasons or because they are tired of problems that won't go away.

When problems within a marriage are not addressed, they can grow and grow like weeds in summer that take over a garden if left unattended. After a while, you can't even find the vegetables because it's so overgrown with destructive weeds. Avoidance of personal or relationship problems never solves anything but rather tends to blow things entirely out of proportion so that it looks like the only avenue left is escape. How better to sabotage a relationship than adultery? The problem is that it doesn't fix anything, it just leads to more difficult issues. Whatever the problems in your marriage, avoidance is not the answer.

What Do Cheaters Feel?

Most often adulterers feel overwhelmed with guilt for their actions. They are plagued with anxiety, trying desperately to keep their secret safe. They may be feeling trapped and helplessly caught between their lover and their spouse, both demanding things from them. People who are involved in illicit affairs are more likely to engage in unsafe sex, drug and alcohol abuse, or overeating or undereating. On top of that, they may be feeling remorse, wondering how this happened, wondering if there is any way to fix it.

Sounds like a terribly uncomfortable place to be, doesn't it? And the worst part, it is of their own making. They did this to themselves. They blew apart their marriage; they damaged the family unit, and if they have children, their children will pay the price for their actions. They will probably wonder – what was I thinking?

What Does the Betrayed Spouse Feel?

When a spouse first learns of the betrayal, he or she is usually in a state of shock and disbelief. Any trust that existed has been destroyed. They are probably feeling alone, confused, angry, and resentful. The blow to self-esteem can be devastating, making them feel unattractive or undesirable. They are filled with doubts about themselves, wondering what caused their spouse to cheat. Was it something they did? Something they didn't do? Something they should have seen coming? How could they have missed the signs? Why am I not good enough?

They may be feeling shame or even self-blame, humiliation for being duped or deceived, embarrassment that they were so trusting, blaming themselves for not being a better partner. They struggle with anxiety about what comes next, what the future holds, and may fall into depression because of the overwhelming fears about the future and the blow to their self-esteem.

Can the Marriage Survive?

As I said earlier, about 75% of marriages that experience infidelity overcome the blow to their relationship, and that is promising for those who want to save their marriages. What makes the difference between the marriages that survive and the ones that fail?

There are several factors that contribute to the outcome. The most significant factor is the desire to save the marriage, and neither party may fully understand what they want in the beginning of the process. Avoid putting pressure on yourself to make decisions right away. This will just add to your stress and anxiety. You need time to think, time to process your emotions, and time to decide what you want for your future. You need to give each other space, take some time apart to get your bearings.

One of the greatest concerning factors is whether or not emotional attachment is involved and how long the affair has been going on. Obviously, if the adulterer has a strong emotional attachment to their lover and the affair has been lengthy, it will be more difficult to make a complete break and dissolve the relationship. If you hope to save your marriage, if it has any hope of survival, the relationship should be severed immediately.

Children are a major factor in considering whether to save the marriage or not. Divorce is difficult for all parties, but it is probably the most heartbreaking for children. According to an article in *Psychology Today* by Carl E. Pickhardt, Ph.D., "Divorce introduces a massive change into the life of a boy or girl no matter what the age. Witnessing loss of love between parents, having parents break their marriage commitment, adjusting to going back and forth between two different households, and the daily absence of one parent while living with the other, all create a challenging new family circumstance in which to live. In the personal history of the boy or girl, parental divorce is a watershed event. The life that follows is significantly changed from how life was before."[5] Putting your children through this type of tremendous upheaval is gut-wrenching.

Another consideration that plays a huge part in the decision-making process are the financial implications. If one spouse is the main contributor to the family budget, the other spouse is left with the possibility of being poverty-stricken. In some cases where the main caretaker (usually the wife) of the children has not worked for several years, getting back into the workforce may be a daunting task, and it may be difficult to earn enough money to maintain a home with children. If both spouses contributed equally, it will still likely be financially devastating because they will then have to establish and pay for two places of residence and divide all their assets.

When deciding if you want to save your marriage or not, you should be aware that people who have cheated before are three times more likely to cheat again. Those are daunting statistics. In the Bible, in Matthew 5:32, it says,

But I tell you that anyone who divorces his wife, except for sexual immorality, makes her the victim of adultery, and anyone who marries a divorced woman commits adultery.

Based on this scripture, Jesus is saying that divorce is not permissible, except in matters of unfaithfulness. Does this mean that Jesus is saying you should divorce in cases of adultery? No, not at all. He is simply saying that adultery is a valid reason for getting a divorce, but that is only if you cannot repair the marriage.

Marriage is sacred; it was designed and created by God. He takes it seriously, and he expects us to do the same. Marriage should never be ended without careful consideration, and only then after every effort has been made to forgive, reconcile, and repair the bond of marriage. In some cases, this is not possible, but every effort should be made before deciding to divorce. Seeking God in prayer, asking for his wisdom and direction, will help guide through the process of deciding what to do. Nothing will give you more peace and assurance about your choices than allowing God to speak to your heart. Seek him earnestly, and he will give you the wisdom to make the choice that is best for you and your family.

If you are seriously contemplating trying to reconcile, here are some things to consider before you move forward.

- Address the problems in the marriage that contributed to the infidelity; this is a crucial first step. Are the problems fixable? Are both parties willing to work on their issues? Are you both willing to seek out marriage counseling? Seeking out a Christian pro-marriage counselor would be the best choice.

- Is the offending spouse remorseful and willing to take responsibility for the affair and his or her actions? Is the offending spouse willing to be held accountable, promise not to cheat again, and commit to saving the marriage? Do you have any lingering doubts or insecurity about the intentions professed? It will take time to rebuild trust but insisting upon establishing strict guidelines for accountability should help to provide reassurance.

- Acknowledge that there was likely fault on both sides, determine what role each of you played, and be honest about what went wrong. Be willing to be brutally honest with each other and with yourself and keep an open mind.

- To move forward, you will need to work on rebuilding your relationship, develop a sturdier foundation, and make new and stronger connections. Find a new interest or hobby that the two of you can share. Brainstorm about possible options. You may want to engage in two options, one chosen by each of you.

You will need to rebuild your relationship with a new and stronger foundation for your marriage. Building your marriage on the solid rock foundation of Jesus Christ and godly principles will provide the firmest foundation you could hope for. Listen to what Jesus says in Luke 6:46-49 (NLT):

> *"So why do you keep calling me 'Lord, Lord!' when you don't do what I say? I will show you what it's like when someone comes to me, listens to my teaching, and then follows it. It is like a person building a house who digs deep and lays the foundation on solid rock. When the floodwaters rise and break against that house, it stands firm because it is well built. But anyone who hears and doesn't obey is like a person who builds a house right on the ground, without a foundation. When the floods sweep down against that house, it will collapse into a heap of ruins."*

Floods will come and you don't want your house to collapse into a heap of ruins. A marriage based on a godly foundation according to God's wise words of wisdom has a much better chance of survival. Working on rebuilding that foundation and rebuilding trust will take time; it is a process, but you can make the relationship stronger than ever if you are both fully committed to making lasting changes.

Chapter 8 Making It Personal

Has someone close to you experienced the pain and betrayal of adultery?

1. Do you consider online relationships, pornography, and excessive flirting as harmless activities or as a betrayal to your marriage vows? Does your spouse feel the same way?

2. People most often cheat because a need or desire is not being met– a need for intimacy, excitement, respect, admiration, appreciation, affection, etc. Understanding what your spouse needs or expects from you is critically important to avoid a painful betrayal. What basic needs in a marriage relationship are most important to you personally? Is your spouse aware of what is most important to you?

3. Have you ever experienced betrayal from someone you loved or trusted? How did that make you feel? Were you able to restore that relationship? Why or why not?

4. Identify some of the problems in a marriage that can lead to infidelity.

5. After better understanding and identifying the elements that are lacking in a marriage that can lead to infidelity, are there areas in your marriage that may be lacking? If so, what can you do to improve in that area?

6. Do you think that your marriage could survive infidelity? Why or why not?

7. What can you do today to work towards improving your marriage and safeguard against infidelity?

CHAPTER 9

FORGIVENESS

Have you ever felt pain so deep in your soul that you felt like someone put a knife in your gut and kept twisting and turning it? I have. I must admit that I have never actually experienced a knife wound other than that slip of the knife when I was cutting vegetables, but the emotional pain I experienced was so very real and utterly devastating. Not long after the pain came the anger, the overwhelming desire to hurt that other person as much as I was hurting. My emotions were in turmoil – one part of me wanted to give into the rage and lash out, but the other part of me feared what that would do to my family.

We have all been hurt, but the hurt is even more crushing when it comes at the hand of someone you love, especially your spouse. How do you forgive someone who hurt you? Why should you when you know your anger is justified? Why would you want to forgive? What purpose would it serve to let go of the anger and forgive that person? Is it possible to restore a relationship after betrayal? These are the things we will consider in this chapter.

Let's first look at what forgiveness is and what it is not. Forgiveness is the act of forgiving; it is letting go of the right to retaliate, no longer seeking revenge; letting go of the anger and resentment. Forgiveness is a choice, and it is a process. When the hurt cuts deeply, the process can be long and arduous. It takes time and patience.

Forgiving does not mean that the action or the betrayal was acceptable behavior or that you are excusing or condoning what they did or did not do. It does not necessarily mean that you agree to reconcile your relationship with that person. In some circumstances, the relationship may be damaged beyond repair. Only you can decide if the relationship can be restored. It depends on how much you value the relationship; how important it is to you.

In a marriage relationship there is so much more at stake, and the need to forgive is much more compelling even though it may be extremely difficult. You both made a commitment to each other for better or worse. In addition, it may not be just your lives that are at stake, but the lives of your children or other family members who would be deeply impacted. But even if you wanted to forgive, how do you do that when the pain is still there, the hurt hasn't gone away, and every time you see that person your anger flares yet again. How do you forgive?

Forgiveness is a Choice

The choice is yours. Do you want to forgive or not? Remember, at this point, you are not making the choice to reconcile, you are not excusing or condoning the behavior. It is a choice only you can make. In making a choice to let go of the need for revenge, you are also making a choice to let go of the anger.

You may say that you cannot control the anger you feel right now, it is beyond your control, and that may be true, but remember that forgiveness is a process. First you make the choice to forgive and determine that you will move forward and not let the past hurt you anymore. Once you are firm in your decision, then you work on the rest and it will come if you are determined. It requires patience, persistence, and time.

Why Should You Forgive?

So if I want to hold onto my anger, what is the harm? I am just not ready to let go. The pain is too raw and fresh, the hurt is overwhelming. It isn't fair that he or she should get away with what was done. They should be held accountable. These are all valid points, but the bottom line is that holding onto anger can be so extremely damaging to your personal wellbeing - mentally, emotionally, physically, and spiritually. Anger is a negative emotion that can eat you alive.

> *Anger is an acid that can do more harm to the vessel in which it is stored than to anything on which it is poured. - Mark Twain*

The truth is that the anger does more harm to the person who is angry than to the offender. There is an old saying that holding onto anger is like drinking poison and expecting the other person to die. If you want to do what is best for you, you will choose to let go of the anger. You may not be able to let go immediately and feel released from the anger, but remember, it is a process. Taking that first step by deciding to let go of the anger, you are making the best choice for your own wellbeing. In James 1:20, the Bible says,

Anger does not produce the righteousness that God desires.

We need to let it go, especially if we want a right relationship with God. Matthew 16:14-15 tells us,

For if you forgive other people when they sin against you, your heavenly Father will also forgive you. But if you do not forgive others their sins, your Father will not forgive your sins.

I don't know about you, but I am well aware that I need forgiveness from God, and I would rather not hold onto anger that will keep me from receiving God's forgiveness and damage my personal wellbeing. When we hang onto harmful emotions like anger, it is directly contrary to what God desires for us. What are the other benefits of letting go of the anger and forgiving? There are many! When you choose to let go:

- The offending person no longer has power over you; you take your power back when you refuse to be a victim any longer to those negative feelings that are so destructive.

- You have a more positive outlook on life – improved mental health, improved mood, more optimism, higher self-esteem, and peace of mind.

- You have a sense of hope and your ability to experience joy and gratitude improves.

- You protect yourself from the negative feelings that can be so emotionally exhausting, such as depression, anxiety, irritability, and even hostility.

- You decrease your stress level because unresolved anger induces stress.

- You can learn from your experience and subsequently develop more resilience and inner strength that will serve you well in the future.

The choice is yours. You can choose to let go and forgive or not. It is not always easy, but clearly the better choice is to let go of the anger for your benefit and begin the process of forgiveness.

What does God say about holding onto anger and refusing to forgive? In Ephesians 4:31-32, it says,

> *Get rid of all bitterness, rage and anger, brawling and slander, along with every form of malice. Be kind and compassionate to one another, forgiving each other, just as in Christ God forgave you.*

Absolutely no one is perfect, not even you, and especially not me. If we want to be forgiven for the wrong things we have done, we need to be forgiving of each other. You may say, "Well, I haven't done anything nearly as bad as (him or her)." God doesn't make distinctions when it comes to the severity of transgressions. If you refuse to forgive, how can you expect God to forgive you? It is an attitude of the heart. Do you have a prideful heart or one that is humble? If you are judgmental and unforgiving and hardhearted, how can you expect to be treated differently? In Matthew 7:1-2, it says,

> *Do not judge, or you too will be judged. For in the same way you judge others, you will be judged, and with the measure you use, it will be measured to you.*

I don't know about you, but I think I will forgo judging others and seek to develop a heart that is open, forgiving, compassionate, and merciful because I hope to receive the same from God himself.

Steps to Forgiveness

You have (or at least I hope you have) made the decision to forgive. Now what? The first step was making the choice to forgive. Trust me, I know that was not an easy choice, but it is the best choice. The next step is to take a hard look at your anger and evaluate the offense. What did he or she do that made you angry? Get to the root of the anger. Is it linked to another incident from your past? Is it related to a fear that you have? How does the offense make you feel? Do you feel justified in your anger? Are you able to see the situation from his or her perspective? Put yourself in their shoes and consider if and how you would have reacted differently.

Take some time to ponder each of those questions and give yourself permission to accept your feelings and your emotional response. Let that sink into your spirit. You were hurt and it made you angry, you acknowledge how it made you feel, and then, you let it go.

Let go of the anger that leads to bitterness. Let go of the desire to take revenge. Let go of the resentment that can lead to depression. Let go of the victim mentality. Let go of the negativity and toxic feelings. Instead, choose to embrace the positive choice you are making for your wellbeing. You are not forgiving for their benefit; you are forgiving for you. You are releasing it and letting go so that you can be open once again to all that life has to offer you. You are free to choose hope and joy. It all sounds easy, right? Easy to say, harder to actually do it.

I want to caution you here that it is not always easy to let go forever and ever, amen. You may find yourself face to face with this person and a memory of that offense will rear its ugly head causing your anger to flare. Do not be discouraged. We are human and we are susceptible to falling back into old habits or feelings that we would rather not have. The good news is that you can make that choice again and again to let go of that anger as often as you need. Remind yourself that it is for your benefit that you made the decision to let it go. It is the enemy of your soul that throws that old hurt in your face, so ask God to help you to let it go. He is faithful and will help you.

The next step is to look for the silver lining. Evaluate what you gained from the experience. Every experience, whether negative or positive, can be of benefit to us as we learn new things, grow in maturity, and build strength and character. What did you learn from this experience? What would you do differently? How have you grown from this? Do you feel wiser, more resilient, stronger? I pray that you do.

The final step may be the hardest step – reconciliation. In some relationships, a reconciliation is not always possible or desirable, but in a marriage relationship this is the desirable outcome in most cases.

Reconciliation

Again, it goes back to how much do you value the relationship? Ultimately, the choice is yours, but how much is at stake? If the relationship is not restored, what are the implications? Who else will be hurt? What would be the fallout? How would it impact you and those you care about emotionally, physically, financially, and spiritually? These are all important aspects to consider. You cannot rush the process. You need to take your time and think it through.

Be very honest with yourself as you evaluate the pros and cons of reconciliation. You need to thoughtfully consider and understand what you expect and what you need for the future of the relationship to be successful. Here are some questions that you may want to ask yourself:

- Did the offense cross any of your personal boundaries? Did your spouse know about the boundaries or was he or she blindsided by your angry reaction? What boundaries need to be established moving forward? Is there any room for compromise?

- What do you need from your partner? Are your needs being met? Are your needs realistic and reasonable? Have you shared your needs with your partner? Strange as it may sound, mindreading is not a prerequisite for a successful relationship – you must communicate your needs and desires.

- What behaviors caused or led up to the problem between you? Honestly consider if your own behavior contributed to the problem in some way. If so, are you willing to make the necessary changes to bridge the gap between you?

- How has this experience changed you? How has it impacted your partner? Did you learn something that will help you build a stronger relationship?

If you make the decision to reconcile (and I hope you do!), you both need to talk it out – discuss what went wrong, what other factors were involved, what needs to change, what needs to stay the same. Review and talk about the questions above to ensure that you understand each other, understand what went wrong, why it happened, and what will keep it from happening again. You may need to go back and look at the chapter on Communication and determine if there are some areas that you need to work on together.

One final thing I want to say on reconciliation – in any relationship, especially in a marriage relationship, a spirit of unity is essential to making it work. Without unity, there is no sense of peace. You need to understand that you are in this together, you need to be united in purpose and love. In Ephesians 4:2-3, it says,

> *Be completely humble and gentle; be patient, bearing with one another in love.*
> *Make every effort to keep the unity of the Spirit through the bond of peace.*

When we are forgiven by God, when we forgive others, when we are forgiven by others, it will boost your joy, it will relieve the heavy burden you have been carrying and you will feel light and free. Unity of the heart and unity of the spirit is what God desires for you and your marriage.

Don't just settle for staying together and tolerating each other. You were both designed to be in a relationship that brings joy, fulfillment, and thanksgiving. Never let that flame of love die out or grow dim. Work at it to rekindle the love and devotion that prompted you to join your lives together in the first place. Having a loving, caring, thriving relationship is priceless!

Chapter 9 Making It Personal

We all do things we regret, especially as young men and women. What is the dumbest thing you ever did as a teenager?

1. What is the definition of forgiveness? What does it mean to forgive someone?

2. What is NOT necessarily part of the forgiving process?

3. What does God say about refusing to forgive others?

4. Why is it harmful to hang onto anger? How is it detrimental to your wellbeing?

5. What are some of the benefits of letting go of the anger?

6. Is there someone that you have wronged or hurt who has forgiven you? If so, how did that feel? How did it impact your relationship? If not, have you ever considered righting that wrong by apologizing and asking for forgiveness?

7. Is there someone you are having a difficult time forgiving? If so, how has that impacted your life? What would it look like if you forgave that person – how would it impact your life, your relationship?

8. In a marriage relationship, we may either consciously or unconsciously hold onto feelings of hurt or anger long after the event, and even if it may seem small and insignificant, it is still there, hidden under the surface. Is there some unresolved issue or feeling that you are holding onto that may be causing you to feel resentment or bitterness? If so, you need to bring it out into the open, deal with it, and put it to rest once and for all.

CHAPTER 10

FINANCIAL HARMONY

Financial concerns can put a severe strain on a marriage. In fact, statistics show that over half of the couples who got divorced within the last five years have stated that finances played a significant role in the decision to end the marriage. What does that mean to you? It means that if you can find a way to compromise and agree on how to handle your finances, it will result in a healthier marriage relationship. To cultivate that healthier relationship, first and foremost, you need to both have a healthy relationship with money.

Consider the role that money plays in your life. We all need it to exist – to put a roof over our heads, food in our mouths, and clothes on our backs, among other things. But what is your personal view of money in relation to the place it holds in your life? Does money have a hold on your heart, on your soul? God warns us in 1 Timothy 6:10,

> *For the love of money is the root of all kinds of evil. And some people, eager for money, have wandered from the true faith and pierced themselves with many griefs.*

Money is not evil, but the LOVE of money is the root of all kinds of evil. The love of money can cause people to do some terrible things. If you love money more than God or more than your family, I think it is safe to say that you don't have a healthy relationship with money. To have a healthy relationship with money, money must be viewed in the proper perspective. Your money is a blessing from God. The Bible says that everything good in our lives comes from God. James 1:17 states,

> *Every good and perfect gift is from above, coming down from the Father of the heavenly lights, who does not change like shifting shadows.*

Money, along with all other blessings, is a gift from God. We are blessed, sometimes with barely enough to squeak by or sometimes with an abundance, but ultimately, our money is a gift from God. We are entrusted with money to use to satisfy our needs. Our money actually belongs to God. We are more like managers of the money we have been given, and we are expected to manage it wisely. What does God expect from us as managers? The Bible has quite a bit to say about money and how to use it.

Budgeting and Planning

Keeping good records, developing a budget, planning ahead, and having goals are all important aspects of good money management. We are encouraged to keep good records. Proverbs 27:23 says,

> *Be sure you know the condition of your flocks, give careful attention to your herds;*

Now most of us do not have flocks or herds, but in Biblical times, their flocks were often their most valuable possession. They were encouraged to be aware of how the flock was doing and paying careful attention to maintaining their herds. Keeping good records is a key component of developing a budget and a plan.

I recently needed to gather important documents for my elderly mother to apply for benefits on her behalf. I was amazed at her extensive record keeping and how it made my job so much easier. All the important documents were neatly filed away by category, everything in its proper place. It made what could have been a horrendous ordeal into a very manageable task. It is worth the small amount of effort it takes to get organized and keep a good accounting of what you have and what you have spent – especially at tax time!

Developing a budget helps you to better understand what you have to work with, what you need to maintain your needs and pay your bills, what you need to prepare for in the future, and what you would like to do with any excess. This area was never my strong point.

Managing the money in our household was always one of my responsibilities, simply because my husband did not want to do it. I kept good records, balanced the checkbook, and was careful when spending money, but I never sat down and planned a budget. Our family survived, but, in retrospect, I think I would have stressed a whole lot less over money if I had taken the time to develop a budget. Money is not meant to cause stress, and in most cases, if you manage it properly, everything eventually falls into place. Developing a budget does not make managing money stress-free, but it certainly helps to make it less stressful.

Please don't misunderstand, I am well aware that at times there is no getting around it – managing money can be stressful, especially if there is not enough to meet your needs and pay the bills. There can be unexpected expenses that come up, an unexpected increase in costs, or income you counted on that disappeared. So many people have experienced that during the pandemic when lucrative jobs were suddenly deemed "nonessential" and there was no income. So many people struggled just to put food on the table. When things like this happen, this is when your faith needs to fill the gap, but we will discuss this later in this chapter.

Planning is essential. Setting limits and boundaries is essential. Proverbs 21:5 (NLT) says,

> *Good planning and hard work lead to prosperity, but hasty shortcuts lead to poverty.*

If we work hard and plan well, we will be prosperous. However, we need to be patient and not jump ahead. In this age of instant gratification – I see it, I deserve it, I want it now – it can be a struggle to be patient, but it is crucial to develop a plan and have the patience to see it through. Other words of wisdom can be found in Luke 14:28-30, we are told,

> *Suppose one of you wants to build a tower. Won't you first sit down and estimate the cost to see if you have enough money to complete it? For if you lay the foundation and are not able to finish it, everyone who sees it will ridicule you, saying, 'This person began to build and wasn't able to finish.'*

Jumping ahead too soon is foolish and can lead to ruin. Take your time, set your priorities, and avoid debt whenever possible. Of course, if you want to own a home or a car, you will likely incur some debt, but make sure that you do not get in over your head. Avoid impulse buying and pay off your credit cards every month to avoid paying high interest rates. There are some wise words in Proverbs 22.7:

The rich rule over the poor, and the borrower is a slave to the lender.

A long time ago I heard a saying that really stuck with me - take care that your possessions don't own you, but rather that you own your possessions. Be careful that you do not become indebted to stuff. If you incur too much debt, it may feel like you are just constantly working to pay bills with no time to enjoy your possessions.

Tithing

What is tithing? Tithing is our way of giving back a portion, or one-tenth, to God for those things that he has blessed us with. Giving of our money, our time, and our talents is what is expected of us as Christ-followers. Proverbs 3.9 says,

> *Honor the Lord with your wealth, with the first fruits of all your crops.*

We give generously out of our love for God, to provide money needed to spread the gospel and maintain the necessary ministries of the church. We are to give freely. In 2 Corinthians 9:7, Paul says,

> *Each of you should give what you have decided in your heart to give, not reluctantly or under compulsion, for God loves a cheerful giver.*

When you give generously with a joyful heart, God blesses you for it. In Malachi 3:10, we are told,

> *"Bring the whole tithe into the storehouse, that there may be food in my house. Test me in this," says the Lord Almighty, "and see if I will not throw open the floodgates of heaven and pour out so much blessing that there will not be room enough to store it.*

God encourages us to test him in this area. He challenges us to give and see if he doesn't bless us with so much more than we give. If you have never tithed before, you may need to work up to giving a tenth of your income, but I would encourage you to give generously and even sacrificially. You will see that God will bless you for it!

Saving

When we were first married, we lived paycheck to paycheck, especially after the kids came along. Saving money each month was tough, and I must admit that we did not save much in the beginning. But making a habit of regularly putting money aside is essential for financial stability because emergencies do happen and being prepared lessens stress. Starting that habit, even if it is only $10 a week, is a habit worth keeping for a lifetime. Sean Covey, a very successful businessman, author, and inspirational speaker says,

> *Depending on what they are, a habit will either make us or break us. We become what we do repeatedly.*

How true! Get into the habit of saving and tithing regularly, and I promise that you will be extremely glad you did. Proverbs 20:21 tells us,

> *The wise have wealth and luxury, but fools spend whatever they get.*

Don't be foolish, make wise decisions that lead to financial stability and enjoy more freedom and less stress. The other benefit is that making good financial decisions will make a positive impact on the health of your marriage relationship.

Contentment and Gratitude

Learning to be content in all circumstances is a gift of immeasurable value, especially regarding your finances. There will always be someone with a bigger house, a fancier car, and more expensive clothes, going on more fabulous vacations. If you try to keep up, you will never be satisfied, you will always be stressed, and you will never be happy. Does that sound like something you want for your life? I know it's tempting to want all of those things, but it is just not worth going into debt over. In 1 Timothy 6:6-7, it says,

> *Yet true godliness with contentment is itself great wealth. After all, we brought nothing with us when we came into the world, and we can't take anything with us when we leave it. So if we have enough food and clothing, let us be content.*

Wise words, indeed! Instead of laboriously working towards gaining material things that only satisfy for a short time, learning to be content and being grateful for what we have is worth more than gold. Ecclesiastes 6:9 (NLT) says,

> *Enjoy what you have rather than desiring what you don't have. Just dreaming about nice things is meaningless—like chasing the wind.*

Meaningless pursuits are a waste of time and energy. Cultivating an attitude of thanksgiving brings joy and contentment, giving into greed breeds frustration and dissatisfaction. God has so much to say about this subject, so please allow me to share just one more verse. Ecclesiastes 5:19 (NLT) says,

> *And it is a good thing to receive wealth from God and the good health to enjoy it. To enjoy your work and accept your lot in life—this is indeed a gift from God.*

Enjoy what you have, give thanks to God for your many blessings, and be happy!

Love and Compromise

You and your spouse are two different people and you both have different ideas, different needs, different wants, and different desires. You will not always agree on how the money should be spent. The fundamental principle here is to put your love and the health of your relationship first before anything that you may want to spend money on.

Here again, learning to put your spouse's needs above your own is the key to success and happiness in your relationship. Proverbs 15:17 (NLT) says,

> *A bowl of vegetables with someone you love is better than steak with someone you hate.*

How true is that! It is vital that you make important financial decisions together. Communication plays a significant role here too. Discuss the reasons why you each think the expenditure is a good idea or not. Listen carefully to your spouse with an open mind and talk about the pros and cons. Do your best to understand and accept what your spouse wants or needs, and he or she should do the same for you. Consider this verse from 1 Corinthians 13:4-5 (NLT),

> *Love is patient and kind. Love is not jealous or boastful or proud or rude. It does not demand its own way. It is not irritable, and it keeps no record of being wronged.*

Love does not demand its own way. If one of you is very much against spending money on something, is it worth the damage it may do to your relationship? Is the expenditure ultimately going to benefit your family or just you?

Every couple faces decisions and conflicts about money. I tend to spend money on little things – clothes, household items, decorative items, shoes (I have way too many shoes), and flowers. In the summer, I love to surround myself with an extravagant display of flowers. Our back porch looks like a nursery in the summer. My expenditures do not usually amount to much more than $100 or so.

My husband on the other hand, spends money on big things. He has an expensive hobby restoring old cars. He worked hard all his life, so I don't begrudge him spending money on his hobby as long as it is within reason. Most of the time he makes decent investments in the cars, but there were two that I objected to him buying that he bought anyway – one turned out to be a loss and the other will likely prove to be a "barely break even" investment. I try not to take too much pleasure in the fact that I was right, but it is tough to refrain from saying, "I told you so."

In most relationships, there is usually one who tends to be more of a saver and the other more of a big spender. Hopefully, this provides balance in the relationship regarding financial stability. If you were both big spenders, you may be more prone to experiencing financial difficulties. If you tend to be the big spender, listen to your spouse's concerns and carefully weigh the pros and cons of the expense. Consider how it will impact your finances and how it will impact your relationship. Do this before you commit to spending the money and you may be able to avoid costly mistakes.

However, there may be times in your marriage when you or your spouse makes a bad investment – it happens. No one is perfect, we all make mistakes. It may put a strain on your relationship causing hurt and angry feelings that are difficult to let go of. It may take time to repair the damage done to the relationship. In cases like this, the offender needs to take responsibility for his or her careless disregard for damage caused by apologizing and doing whatever it takes to make amends. You both need to find a way to move past it.

The bottom line is this – you won't always agree on where money should be spent. There will be times when your spouse spends money on something you disagree with or even strongly object to, but your relationship must be the first priority. It needs to be more important than the money or being right. You are in this together and you need to find a way back to a thriving healthy relationship or neither of you will be happy. Remember those wedding vows? For richer or poorer. Forgiveness is not the easy way, but it is the best way to repair the relationship.

Determining how to manage finances appropriately is not an easy task and agreeing on this topic is harder still. If you are struggling in this area, I would strongly suggest investing time into taking a financial course such as Dave Ramsey Financial Peace University (A Proven Plan for Financial Success | RamseySolutions.com). This resource helps you to understand from a Christian perspective how to manage your money successfully. Some local churches offer classes for financial management help. Another option would be to seek professional counseling to help you find a way to work through this issue together. Whatever option you choose, take that step of faith towards better financial stability – you won't regret it!

Chapter 10 Making It Personal

Who is responsible for managing the finances in your relationship?

1. Money is a blessing and a reward for our hard work and wisdom, and it is provided for our life-sustaining needs. All blessings are a gift from God, including money. When we acknowledge that our wealth is a gift from God, that it comes from God and belongs to God, it puts money in the proper perspective. Is this a difficult viewpoint for you to accept? Why or why not?

2. Have you ever been caught unprepared for a money emergency? Share your experience. What could you have done differently? Are you better prepared for emergencies now?

3. We are instructed to keep good records and develop a plan (or a budget) and goals for our money. Do you work off a budget or just wing it? How does that work for you? Do you think your style of financial management works well for you or could it be improved? What could you do to make improvements?

4. Tithing is a fundamental principle of the Christian faith. Do you believe in tithing? What is your experience with tithing? Have you ever "tested" God in giving as he challenges in Malachi 3:10?

5. What is your habit regarding saving money? Do you feel confident that you have enough money saved for emergencies? Do you feel confident that you will have enough money when it comes time to retire? If not, what can you do to feel more confident?

6. Have you ever bought something major against your spouse's wishes or without consulting your spouse? How did that work out for you? In retrospect, would you have done things differently?

7. Has your spouse ever bought something major without consulting you or against your wishes? How did that work out? Have you talked about how you can avoid future conflicts about spending?

8. On a scale of 1 (not content at all) to 10 (very content), how would you rate your personal level of contentment? Do you think that as you have matured you are more content than you used to be?

CHAPTER 11
CHILDREN CHANGE THINGS

hildren are truly a gift from God, a blessing beyond measure. They bring joy and a sense of fulfillment into your life. They are wondrous little creatures that capture your heart in a way that is difficult to comprehend.

In Psalm 127:3-5 (NLT), the Bible says,

Children are a gift from the LORD;
they are a reward from him.
Children born to a young man
are like arrows in a warrior's hands.
How joyful is the man whose quiver is full of them!

Children create a special bond between the mother and father that never goes away. The parents are always and forever joined together in that relationship with their child or children. You are bound together in purpose to raise this little bundle of joy together as a team, to love and nurture him or her forever, but it comes at a cost.

Introducing a child into a romantic and/or a marriage relationship definitely, absolutely, without a doubt, will change the dynamics of that relationship. You need to know that going in, expect it, accept it, and learn how to adapt and adjust to the changes. It is not your fault or your partner's fault, it just is.

Most people say that children are the most rewarding part of life, and I have definitely found that to be true, but parenting is stressful. The demands on your time, your money, and your energy are significant. The dynamics of the relationship changes as soon as you learn you are going to be parents, and it continues to change and evolve throughout the rest of your lives. You have both taken on new roles as parents along with the responsibilities that incurs. The rewards are wonderful, but the challenges are not for those who are faint of heart.

Your children will be dependent on you for the next two decades, and even when they become independent, the concern for their wellbeing never goes away. Don't misunderstand, I wholeheartedly believe that children are worth every sacrifice, but I also believe that parents need to be prepared for what comes next and to know that they are not alone in their struggles.

Change in Perspective

So now you are going to be parents – what changes can you expect in the beginning of this miraculous journey? I think the most profound difference is how you see the world. Your perspective changes. Your priorities change. Your vision for your future changes. You see the world through the eyes of a parent, and it is different. It is hard to describe the shift – it is something you need to experience for yourself, but it is a profound difference.

You are now responsible for this helpless little being who will look to you for love, protection, food, clothing, shelter, and all the other necessities of life. You don't get days off as a parent, the job is 24 hours a day, 7 days a week. You may get a break now and again when you delegate your responsibility to a babysitter or your spouse for a time, but ultimately, you are the one in charge of this little person.

You and your spouse make the decisions and choices that critically impact the future of your child. No matter how hard you try, you will not always get it right. The only thing we can do is try to do the best we know how, pray for guidance, and love them. If you do that, your child will not only survive, but your child will thrive.

Managing the Responsibilities

Along with your new responsibilities come the decisions about how you and your partner will divide the duties of parenthood. Sleep becomes a very precious commodity and can sometimes prove to be very elusive, which tends to increase irritability. Then there is the continuous cycle of needs – feedings every few hours, diapers to be changed, a lot more laundry, bottles to prepare, and soothing the child who seems to cry all the time. Mothers will also experience out of balance hormones that are beyond their control. You will both need to develop a higher level of patience and understanding for each other and for your child as you figure out how to meet the increased demands of parenthood.

Once again, communication is a key component. If you are feeling overwhelmed or struggling to keep up with the demands, share your thoughts and feelings. You are in this together. You are there to support and encourage each other, but that won't happen if you don't tell your spouse what you need or how they can help. Try not to be critical but do be honest and keep those lines of communication open. You need each other.

Stress of Motherhood

In our society, the brunt of the responsibility for daily care falls on the mother, and she is generally called upon to make the most sacrifices. Mothers who choose to stay home with their child will often feel disconnected from the outside world, a sense of social isolation. As a woman who loved being a mother, I must say that I still really missed the affirmations that I received at work, the compliments on a job well done, and the interaction with my peers.

If your wife put her career on hold for the sake of motherhood, she may experience some blows to her self-worth or self-esteem, especially if her sense of purpose was connected to her professional life. If she makes the decision to go back to work after her maternity leave, it is a real struggle to find a healthy balance between being a wife and a mother, while holding down a demanding job. In most cases, when the time comes to go back to work, the majority of the responsibility for care is still on the woman. If the child is sick and needs to see a doctor or the babysitter gets sick or bails at the last minute, it is typically up to the mother to take care of the problem. Challenging indeed!

Dads, it is in your best interest to be proactive and look for ways that you can reduce the stress and the strain your spouse is experiencing. Most of you are aware of the old saying, "If momma ain't happy, ain't nobody happy!" Take heed – that is so true. Take care of the mother of your child, and you will reap the benefits.

When we put the needs of others above our own needs, we are not only pleasing God, but we are making the world a better place. In Philippians 2:2-4, it says,

> *Make my joy complete by being like-minded, having the same love, being one in spirit and of one mind. Do nothing out of selfish ambition or vain conceit. Rather, in humility value others above yourselves, not looking to your own interests but each of you to the interests of the others.*

Put yourself in your partner's shoes and ask yourself what would you need if your positions were reversed? What would it take for you to be encouraged or feel supported? That goes both ways for both partners in the relationship. Being like-minded, being united in purpose, and looking after each other's interests is the ideal approach to parenthood and can lead to a much deeper love relationship.

Financial Concerns

Fathers will often feel more pressure to maintain a stable financial environment for the family. It is quite common to be stressed over the new financial responsibilities. There may be additional medical bills or hospital bills from the birth. There will be additional expenses of diapers, formula, babysitters or childcare, and baby equipment (crib, car seat, stroller, changing table, etc.). There may be the loss of the mother's income during maternity leave or beyond that if she is planning to be a stay-at-home mom. It may be necessary to find housing that has more room to accommodate a family or to live in a better neighborhood with good schools.

According to most statistics, the average cost of raising a child from birth to age 18 is approximately $300,000. That figure does not account for inflation, and that does not include college which can cost anywhere from $10,000 to $35,000 per year. The average college career is four years ($40,000 to $140,000), and it is even more costly for graduate school. It is easy to see why there is an increase in stress over financial concerns when raising a family. The good news is that you don't have to pay for college right away. You will have plenty of time to figure that out. Moms, you need to be aware of the pressure that Dads may be experiencing and help them to find an appropriate balance between work and home responsibilities.

Worries

Honestly, my intention is not to scare you into not having children, but I believe that if you are better prepared, you will have a much more joyful experience and you will feel more successful as you dive into parenting. Whatever concerns or reservations you may have, entrust them to God. He is certainly willing and able to provide the help and guidance you need. In Philippians 4:6-7, it tells us,

> *Do not be anxious about anything, but in every situation, by prayer and petition, with thanksgiving, present your requests to God. And the peace of God, which transcends all understanding, will guard your hearts and your minds in Christ Jesus.*

Don't hesitate to take every concern or worry you have to God in prayer, no matter how small, and give your needs over to him. He will provide all that you need and give you the peace of mind that you so desperately desire.

Romantic vs. Practical Relationship

Another change you will surely notice is that your sex life isn't what it used to be. Mom needs to have time for her body to heal after the birth, but even after you get the green light from the obstetrician, there may be some pain or discomfort. Be patient.

Remember what I said about sleep being a precious commodity? Well, one of you or maybe both of you will find that the desire to sleep often overrides the desire to indulge in sex. Or just when you think the time is finally right, you hear the baby start to cry. That can be a real mood killer.

You are both trying to cope with these changes in your relationship, and it will get better. But "time for us" in the beginning is particularly challenging. Your cute and flirty little conversations will probably be replaced by sharing to-do lists. But as you both adjust and adapt to the changed circumstances, your romantic relationship will resume even better than before if you both make it a priority when the time is right. My best advice is to be patient and be considerate of each other.

Managing Expectations

As parents we try to do our best to raise our children to become independent and valuable members of society. There is no such thing as the perfect parent or the perfect child (more about that in the next chapter), so we need to manage and adjust our expectations of ourselves and our children whenever necessary. Did you hear what I said? There is no such thing as a perfect parent – it is a myth, a fairytale that has no connection to reality. Even with the best intentions, we all fall short.

When I was a new first-time mother, I did my best to be prepared for my new role as a parent. I read the latest and most popular books on pregnancy and motherhood and parenting. I determined what I thought was the best approach to raising a child and intended to stick to the plan that seemed to make the most sense to me. How could I go wrong? One of the most difficult challenges that I was not prepared for was colic – the constant crying and vomiting.

According to the Mayo Clinic, "Colic is frequent, prolonged and intense crying or fussiness in a healthy infant. Colic can be particularly frustrating for parents because the baby's distress occurs for no apparent reason and no amount of consoling seems to bring any relief. These episodes often occur in the evening when parents themselves are often tired."[4] Let me tell you that this was not what I thought I was signing up for as a mother. The incessant crying was driving me mad.

I was exhausted. I was existing on about an average of one to two hours of sleep at the most at one time. As soon as my tiny little son fell asleep, I would lay down and try to sleep, but it wasn't that easy. Exhausted as I was, I was so tense that I couldn't fall asleep. I kept lying there waiting and expecting the crying to start again any second. When I finally did fall asleep, it wasn't long after when I was woken with the sound of crying, again. I felt like such a failure as a mom. I could not figure out how to make this child quit crying and was feeling guilty because I just wanted to be left alone to sleep.

It wasn't until years later when my son was tested for allergies that we discovered he was lactose intolerant, which was most likely the reason for the prolonged bouts of crying and the vomiting. I was breastfeeding, so I mistakenly assumed that it wasn't the breast milk upsetting his stomach. What I didn't know is that when I would drink milk, it would pass that through to my son who could not tolerate it. I definitely got that part wrong.

The good news is that he finally stopped crying and vomiting so much when he was about four months old. It was a really rough beginning, but we survived. Even with the best intentions, we sometimes get it wrong, and that is okay. God knows we are not perfect, and He forgives us because He is the God of great compassion and grace. We need to accept that we are not perfect and give ourselves some grace for the mistakes we will make as parents.

Chapter 11 Making It Personal

What is your first memory as a child?

1. What was your childhood like growing up? Would you describe it as wonderful, average, rough, or extremely dysfunctional? Why?

2. Do you have children, or would you like to have children? Why or why not?

3. What would you do the same as your parents did? What would you do differently?

4. If you are parents, what type of struggles did you experience after the birth of your child? Was it a lot different than you expected? What could you have done differently to make it easier?

5. If you are not yet parents, what do you think you could do to prepare yourself for your child's birth?

6. What is your biggest fear or concern about being a parent?

7. Philippians 4:6-7 says, "Do not be anxious about anything, but in every situation, by prayer and petition, with thanksgiving, present your requests to God. And the peace of God, which transcends all understanding, will guard your hearts and your minds in Christ Jesus." Most people struggle with worrying to some degree; it is just a matter of how much. Do you struggle excessively with worrying? If so, has prayer helped to relieve some of your concerns?

8. Take some time to pray for each other – to relieve any parenting concerns you may have and to fully experience the joys of parenting.

CHAPTER 12

YOUR INFLUENCE

What are your hopes and dreams for your children? If you are like most people, you have visions of what you hope your child will be like when they are grown. Perhaps you envision a successful businessman with a family and a home in the suburbs. Maybe you envision your daughter living in the city and becoming an entrepreneur with a thriving business. Maybe you see your children following in your footsteps choosing a career path similar to yours. Maybe you just want them to grow into responsible adults with a happy family life.

Whatever your dreams and aspirations for your children, you will both play a huge role in determining who they will become as they grow into adulthood. You will have more influence over your children than any other adult in the formative years. That can be good or that can be scary, depending on your perspective. In most cases, it is a mixture of both.

No matter what your perspective, it is always best if you and your spouse present a united front. Talk about your hopes for your children. Discuss how you were each brought up and think about the positive and negative aspects. What values, beliefs, and character traits do you hope to pass on to your children? Identify the common threads, build on those, and try to find ways to compromise on any areas where you have different perspectives. As I have said before, you are in this together. You will do your best work as a team.

Your influence will have a tremendous impact on your children's future. With God's help and the support of each other, you have a significantly better chance of raising children you will be proud of for the rest of your lives. However, let me add a bit of a disclaimer here. Sometimes, even when you do everything right, your child has his or her own free will to go down the wrong path and may cause you serious heartache. There are no guarantees in life, and bad things can and do happen because of the sin in our world.

There will be rough patches and there may be times, especially when they hit those teenage years, you wonder if they will ever straighten out, but trust in the promises of God. He is faithful. Even if you have a rebellious child who insists on taking a destructive path, God will give you the strength to make it through the hardship and times of heartache. Lean on him, pray for your child without ceasing, and entrust him or her into the hands of God.

Our middle child was one that had to test everything. If you would tell him not to touch the stove because it is hot, he would touch it just to see how hot it really was. When he was a teenager, that personality trait led to some difficult years, and we wondered if we would survive or if he would survive! He eventually turned his life around, and we are so grateful for that, because we are well aware that this is not always the case. Your influence matters; your prayers matter. Trust in God and trust in the things that you teach your children. I love the verse from Proverbs 22:6 that says,

> *Start children off on the way they should go, and even when they are old, they will not turn from it.*

Again, this is not a guarantee, but it is an encouragement that we can and do make a difference in the lives of our children. So what can you do to be a positive influence? There are primarily three basic ways that parents influence their children.

Your Example

The first and most obvious way that you influence your child is through your example. Children learn about life and how to live it from you. They develop concepts about how, when, where, and why things should be done based on their familial experiences. They model their ideas and beliefs based on the experiences that you share with them or guide them through. The old adage, "do what I say, not what I do" doesn't really work well with parenting. Kids are smart, and if they see you do something or say something you shouldn't, don't be surprised if you see your behaviors echoed by your children. And of course, they always do or say these things at the most inappropriate times.

We all make mistakes, do things or say things we shouldn't, but that isn't the end of the story. When we mess up, we can tell our children that we are not perfect, and even though we try our best, we sometimes don't get it right. That is the reality of parenting. Let them know that what you did or said was wrong and ask for their forgiveness. This will help them to realize that we all make mistakes, we are not perfect, and we don't expect them to be perfect. The important lesson here is to admit your mistakes, own up to them, and try to do better next time.

I remember one example when I really lost my cool. My oldest son was (and still is) quite stubborn and potty training was one of the most frustrating things I ever dealt with as a mother. It took months, but we finally got the urinating in the toilet part down pat, but the poop was a different matter. After many weeks of frustrating failures, I was beginning to think poopy diapers were never going to go away. He was almost three and a half years old! I diligently followed of the advice of the parenting books – be calm, be encouraging, be forgiving of accidents, be patient, and never yell. Until I didn't.

One afternoon, he was playing with his toys in the bathtub. I left him alone for a few minutes to fold some clothes in the next room. During my absence, he pooped in the bathtub and decided to use it as fingerpaint. Imagine walking into the bathroom and seeing poop smeared all over the tub, the walls, and the toys. My teeth clenched, I tried to remain calm, and said, "What did you do? You are supposed to poop in the potty!" He just looked at me with his big blue eyes and didn't say a word. I cleaned him up and dried him off. He looked at me and said, "Now can we go back to diapers?"

Something snapped inside of me, my frustration had peaked, and self-preservation took over. I took him by the hand, still naked, and dragged him all through the house collecting all of the diapers that were scattered everywhere – in the bathroom, the bedroom, the car in the garage, the diaper bag – and made a great show of loading them into a garbage bag and putting them in the trash can. Then I admit, I yelled at him in quite a loud voice, "We are NEVER going back to diapers. YOU are going to go in the potty, mister, or else. No other options! NO MORE DIAPERS!"

Believe it or not, we hit a turning point that day, and he was suddenly "potty-trained." I guess he finally realized that I meant business. Surely, I could have made my point without dragging him around the house butt naked and hysterically yelling at him, but I had reached my breaking point. I apologized later for losing my temper, but sometimes it just happens. Apologizing lets your child know that you are not perfect and need to be forgiven on occasion, and it models for your children how they should deal with their own mistakes or bad behavior.

Moral Values

Another way that you can influence your children is by sharing your personal code of ethics. You have formed your own belief system about what is right and wrong, and you have developed moral values that you live by or strive to live by. You will have many opportunities to share these values with your children every day by taking advantage of those teachable moments that pop up. You can just tell your child that this is the way we do it because I said so; or you can tell your child this is how we do it and this is why we do it this way.

Let me give an example. Your daughter is playing with her three friends in the family room, and you notice that she and one friend are ridiculing the other friend, who runs out of the room and out the backdoor crying. You can tell your daughter and her friend that they shouldn't do that and express your displeasure; or you can take advantage of a teachable moment. Ask why they were being mean. Ask them how they would feel if the situation were reversed. Explain why the behavior is unacceptable. Explain the consequences of hurting someone else's feelings. Then insist that they apologize because that is what you do when you hurt someone. Taking advantage of these opportunities, you can mold and shape your child's moral values. This will help them to develop their own code of ethics based on the principles you have taught them. Having solid moral values will equip them to make good choices, develop positive relationships, and become good, kind, responsible adults.

More than once, I have been in a store and the clerk makes a mistake giving me too much change. You can either pocket the money pretending you didn't notice and hope the clerk doesn't have to pay the shortage out of his own pocket, or you can say, "Excuse me, but you gave me $5 too much." This shows your child that you value honesty and your integrity more than the extra $5. It also shows your child that even when he can get away with something he knows is wrong, he should instead do the right thing, even if no one is looking. That's what God expects of us. In Titus 2:7 (NLT), we are instructed to model integrity by doing good works of every kind. It says,

> *And you yourself must be an example to them by doing good works of every kind. Let everything you do reflect the integrity and seriousness of your teaching.*

You have a responsibility to teach your children good moral values, and it is to your advantage to do so. If children are taught from a young age to value honesty, integrity, kindness, generosity, patience, and self-control, your job as a parent will be a little less challenging when they become teenagers. It is never too early to start teaching your child valuable life lessons.

Positive Reinforcement

Everyone, no matter how young or old, likes to hear compliments, receive praise, or be told that they are doing a good job. Encouragement is the action of giving someone support, confidence, or hope. It is persuasion to do or to continue doing something. It is the act of trying to stimulate the development of an activity, state, or belief.

Don't we all love to feel encouraged, love to have our accomplishments and good deeds applauded? If we receive encouragement, it will positively reinforce the behavior. What is positive reinforcement? Positive reinforcement is providing an incentive to repeat a desirable behavior by introducing a desirable or pleasant stimulus after the behavior. When your child feels uplifted or encouraged by your compliments or praise, it becomes more likely that the behavior will be repeated.

Positive reinforcement is such a valuable tool to positively influence your child. Unfortunately, some parents neglect to take advantage of it, which is sad because it can be such a powerful tool. If you catch your child in an act of kindness, encourage that behavior by praising them for it. If your child helps you in the kitchen, acknowledge the good behavior by thanking him for his help. If your child brings home a grade better than the last one, acknowledge the improvement to let him know you see he is trying harder.

Sometimes, we may have to look hard to find something positive, especially if the child is going through one of those more difficult phases, but any type of encouraging word may help to turn things around. Those things that irritate us or frustrate us tend to be more noticeable than the good things and stand out more. It is far easier to criticize our children because they are not living up to our expectations, and sometimes those expectations can be set unreasonably high.

It takes effort to use positive reinforcement, but it is worth more than gold. Be intentional about giving your children the encouragement they need. When your do this for your children, you are supporting their positive efforts, and you are giving them confidence in their abilities. You are promoting the hope that they have to please you, and that they will continue to try to please you, thus rewarding you for your efforts. It is a win/win situation.

Parental Goals

Why should you set goals for parenting? Does that seem unnatural? Shouldn't you just do what you think is right at the time and make decisions as they come. You can do it that way, but there are definite benefits for deciding in advance what your goals are. Developing goals for parenting helps you to identify what type of parents you want to be, what is important to you, and what you each need to do to achieve the desired outcome. Your child's success starts with you, so it makes sense to think this through and be intentional about how you want to proceed.

It also gives you the chance to really talk about your goals with your spouse to make sure you are on the same page. You will probably find areas that you disagree on; that is to be expected. But this gives you the opportunity to talk it out, explain why a particular goal is important to you. Of course, you both need to be flexible and willing to compromise to come together with a plan.

Your goals should be both realistic and achievable. As you gain experience in the parenting realm, you will likely need to go back and tweak some of those goals but laying the basic groundwork can help to avoid future conflicts and misunderstandings. It also helps to have the groundwork laid out so you can periodically evaluate if what you have been doing is on target with the original goals you set forth.

Did I do it this way? No, but you have the benefit of learning from my mistakes. I thank God all the time that my children have grown into mature responsible adults who love God and have made me proud to call them my own, but there were some pitfalls along the way that could have been avoided if I had ever been introduced to this idea of parental goal setting a lot sooner.

An ideal overall goal for raising children is to focus on supporting them in their weaknesses and strengths and empowering them to be their best self through encouragement and affirmation. So how do you do achieve the desired outcomes?

Build Connection

First and foremost, I believe, is building connection with your child. Having a strong close relationship based on availability and being there for the important moments. If you are consistently focused on being accessible and being that dependable adult that they know they can count on, that is key to building a strong, thriving relationship. Nothing says, "I love you," more than giving your child a healthy dose of your valuable time.

Being a good listener will also help to establish that desired close connection. As your child grows and matures, ask them questions about what they think and feel. Let them know that you are interested in what their dreams are and what they wish for. These questions can lead to some fascinating thought-provoking ideas and topics.

Commit to spending quality time with your child, not sitting beside them watching television, but interacting with them on a more personal level, being actively engaged in an activity, a project, or teaching them new skills. As I mentioned before, my husband's hobby is restoring old cars, and he would take our boys out in the garage with him and teach them how to use tools and work on cars from the time they were in grade school, and they loved it.

If you have a hobby, share it with your child. If you like to cook, let your child learn beside you. If you like to knit, encourage your child to do her own simple project. If you like to work in the yard, teach them how to plant a garden. If you are a sports fan, teach them the basics of the game; if you like basketball, go out and shoot hoops together. If you need to clean, hand your child a duster or a sponge – teach them to do chores. Your time is the most valuable gift you can give, share it with your child.

My dad loved sports, especially baseball and golf. I hated the golf, but I often sat with him while he was watching a baseball game and he would patiently explain to me what was going on – why they called it a strike when the batter didn't swing, how many outs to an inning, what a pinch hitter was, and the different types of pitches in baseball. To this day, whenever I see a baseball game on TV, I smile and remember the time my dad spent teaching me about the game, and how much I loved the attention.

Most children will love the attention and will respond with enthusiasm. Take advantage of these opportunities when you can because once your child hits adolescence, the game changes. It is so much harder to develop and maintain that connection if it's not established during the childhood years. It can still be done, but it is so much more challenging.

Another way to build connection is spending time together as a family. Make sharing evening meals a priority to be closely guarded. It can be tough with dad working late, your son going to soccer practice and your daughter going in a different direction for softball practice but try to share meals together as frequently as possible.

As a child growing up, my dad always insisted that our family went to church together, and my husband and I continued this tradition with our children. I am so thankful for this godly legacy handed down from my dad. His faith inspired me, and I attribute my precious relationship with Jesus to my dad's guidance and leading.

My family would also take vacations every summer, and I wanted to do the same for my children. I used to feel a little guilty taking money out of our limited budget for vacations, but looking back, some of our most cherished memories are of events that happened when we vacationed together as a family.

Did you have rituals or traditions as a child? If so, consider keeping those traditions alive by handing them down to your children. If you didn't have much in the way of traditions or rituals, create some. Make it a ritual to take a picture of your child on the first day of school every year and every Christmas in front of the tree. Make Friday night a game night or movie night or pizza night. Have traditional foods or ethnic foods on special holidays. Establish a day on the weekend to do something fun together as a family – go for a walk or a bike ride, go fishing, go swimming, or go to a sporting event together. Every night a bedtime, read a story and teach them to say prayers. Taking the time and making the effort to develop these family rituals or traditions creates that special bond making your family feel more connected.

Sharing Values

We talked earlier about sharing your morals and values with your children and the benefits of taking advantage of teachable moments to reinforce the desired qualities, but I want to expand on this a little bit more. We also talked about how your children learn much of what they retain from watching you and learning from your example. Your children watch your every move, imitate you, and may repeat what you say at the most embarrassing moments.

Children learn from our example, but they also learn from what we teach them. God gave us the Ten Commandments to help us to distinguish between right and wrong, between good and evil. This is a good place to start with teaching your children morals and values that are important to you. As parents, you probably want your children to know and understand that they should not curse or steal or lie or kill, and that they should honor their mother and father. In Deuteronomy 11:18-19, God tells us that we should teach our children his ways.

> *Fix these words of mine in your hearts and minds; tie them as symbols on your hands and bind them on your foreheads. Teach them to your children, talking*

about them when you sit at home and when you walk along the road, when you lie down and when you get up.

We talked about teachable moments – this is what God means by "teach them to your children, talking about them when you sit at home, walk along the road (or drive in the car), when you lie down (or tuck your children in at night and say prayers), and when you get up (at every opportunity)." Make teaching your children part of your normal daily routine. There are plenty of opportunities to teach your children if you look for them.

If you want your child to show respect to authority, you need to model that consistently. If a policeman pulls you over for going over the speed limit, don't start cussing under your breath. Your children are watching. If you were in the wrong, admit it, apologize for breaking the law, and treat the officer with respect.

If your son's teacher took an action that you don't believe was justified, give the teacher the benefit of the doubt, listen to what he has to say, and show respect for his authority. Then if it is warranted, ask to respectfully share your thoughts. If you cannot come to an agreement, either let it go or take it to a higher authority if you must, but remember, your children are watching.

If you want them to have respect for their teachers, the principal, the bus driver, the janitor, and the crossing guards, you need to model that same behavior. When your children are young, this is the time to teach this principle. When your child becomes a teenager and shows no respect for authority, guess what? You are an authority figure too, and you will have a hard time managing a rebellious teenager if he doesn't respect your authority. Those years are challenging enough, so you don't want to make it even more difficult for yourself.

Carefully consider the character traits you would like to see in your children and do your best to model them in all you do. If you want your children to show kindness towards others, generosity with their time and talents, respect for diversity and other races, and have a heart of gratitude, you need to consciously model these qualities consistently. And again, take advantage of those teachable moments when you see opportunities for strengthening your viewpoint and reinforcing those values.

Developing a heart of gratitude is critical to having a happy, cheerful disposition. This is a truly desirable trait because who wants to be around a miserable grump? No one. There was one summer when my oldest son was approaching adolescence. He went through this phase of "everything stinks," "this is boring," "there's nothing to do," "this is stupid." The list went on and on. A grouchy, negative, unattractive creature had grabbed a hold of my sweet boy and made him into a miserable whiner. I was frustrated and extremely irritated by this behavior, and at my wit's end. What should I do with this ungrateful child?

I decided that when we said nighttime prayers, he would have to thank God for at least three things that happened that day before he crawled into bed. At first, it was like pulling teeth to get three things out of him; he had a tough time thinking of anything and then he would come up with stupid stuff like "thank God my brother is not a total moron" just to irritate me. But eventually he started having an easier time of it and would sometimes go on and on if it was a really good day. Now this didn't happen in a week. It took time before I started to see a positive change, but it worked. He was no longer this miserable sullen child – he was happy and grateful, and so was I! Being grateful, counting your blessings, and focusing on the positive events in your life is a proven strategy for lifting your spirits and promoting happiness. Gratitude is strongly associated with greater happiness, and who doesn't want to see their child happy?

Chapter 12 Making It Personal

Have you ever been embarrassed by your children imitating you?

1. What are the positive and negative aspects of how you were raised? How will they shape or impact your parenting style?

2. What values, beliefs, and character traits do you hope to pass on to your children?

3. No parent is perfect, and we all blow it occasionally. Can you share a time when your parents blew it and totally lost their cool? What did you learn from that experience?

4. Have you experienced teachable moments with your children or other children in your life? How did that work out?

5. Do you use positive reinforcement as a parenting tool? If so, give an example.

6. What are your parenting goals? Do they coincide with your spouse's viewpoint?

7. Share examples of how you work towards building a strong connection with your children.

8. What values are important to you for your children to learn? Are there any specific values you would like to work on? How can you effectively teach those values to your children?

CHAPTER 13
PARENTING PLAN

Discipline and Setting Healthy Boundaries

Providing guidelines for behavior and setting healthy boundaries creates structure and predictability for your children, giving them a sense of security and stability. It helps to prepare them to follow rules when they get out into the world and start school. Clearly outlining the rules in your home and the subsequent consequences of breaking those rules is fundamental to having a discipline plan that is advantageous for both you and your children. Children obeying their parents makes for a much more secure and peaceful home, and there is a promise in the Bible that talks about this very subject. In Ephesians 6:1-3, it says,

> *Children, obey your parents in the Lord, for this is right. "Honor your father and mother"—which is the first commandment with a promise—"so that it may go well with you and that you may enjoy long life on the earth.*

In this verse, children are commanded to obey their parents and honor their parents, and here is the promise: *so that it may go well with you and that you may enjoy long life on the earth.* Isn't that what we all want for our children? Another thought to keep in mind is that your children watch and see how you treat your parents. If you hope to have a positive, respectful relationship with your children in your old age, be aware that the behavior you modeled toward elderly parents is going to be what they remember and how they are likely to treat you. Honor your father and mother so that it may go well with you!

Children need boundaries to feel more secure, they need to know that you are the boss, that you are going to be consistent, dependable, and that you care enough to ensure they are following the rules. As children grow and develop, they will try to assert their independence and frequently try to test those established boundaries. You, as the parent, must enforce those boundaries consistently to maintain order and to reassure your child that you are in charge. This allows them to feel more safe and secure. Even though they may fight to the finish, if life is without limits, they will undoubtedly feel a sense of insecurity.

Maintaining those boundaries is beneficial for your children and helps to diminish the arguments, the backtalk, and the conflicts in the long run. If at some point you and your spouse see a need to adjust or change those established boundaries, discuss it with your children and make sure they understand that the rules are changing, why they are changing, and understand the consequences of overstepping the boundaries. As always, communication is a key component in any healthy relationship.

In another scripture in Colossians 3:20, it says,

Children, obey your parents in everything, for this pleases the Lord.

Obedient children please the Lord. I don't know about you, but I wanted my children to have every opportunity to grow up to please the Lord. Teaching and expecting obedience helps your child to learn self-control and self-discipline which promotes feelings of self-confidence and self-esteem. Thus, you are helping your child to be better prepared to step out into the world when it is time. It takes work and diligence to set up a plan and stick to it, but it has great value!

Parenting Styles

Parenting styles refers to the strategies that a parent uses to discipline their children, the way they interact with their children, what they demand of them and how they respond to them. According to psychologists, there are four basic parenting styles: authoritative, authoritarian, permissive, and neglectful.

The **Authoritative** style of parenting is the one that is most desirable for raising a child who grows up to be a happy, healthy, successful adult. The authoritative parent works to create and maintain a strong connection with their child. They make and enforce the rules but explain in advance the consequences of breaking the rules. They use positive parenting strategies such as positive reinforcement, teaching their children right from wrong as a preventive measure, and explain the reasons for the rules and take the child's feelings into account. This style of parenting is what is encouraged and promoted in this book (as you probably guessed). Children with authoritative parents grow up to be responsible adults with strong decision-making skills, and they are confident when expressing their opinions.

The **Authoritarian** style of parenting focuses on making the rules and enforcing those rules to the letter regardless of circumstances. It is "my way or the highway" type of attitude, and children should be "seen and not heard." They tend to dole out punishment rather than discipline, and children have no say in anything. Children who experience this style of parenting tend to be obedient, but poor decision-makers, angry with their parents, and can become hostile angry adults.

The **Permissive** style of parenting sets rules but does little to enforce those rules, subsequently there are no consequences for bad behavior. They don't have much of a positive influence on their children, they are lenient and forgiving, acting more like a friend to the child than a parent. These children tend to struggle in school with academics, have low self-esteem, little self-discipline leading to poor eating habits and sometimes poor hygiene.

The **Uninvolved** or Neglectful style of parenting doesn't make or enforce rules. They do not spend much time with their children and the children basically raise themselves. These parents don't get involved with the child's schoolwork; therefore, the children are usually poor students, have behavioral problems and suffer from low self-esteem. The parents may not be intentionally neglectful but may have mental health issues, suffer from substance abuse, or may not know how to parent.

Not all parents fit neatly into one category, oftentimes they are a mixture of styles or bounce between categories depending on the current situation or circumstances. Oftentimes, one parent is more one category and the other is the opposite, which helps to provide balance. I was an Authoritative parent with Permissive tendencies. My husband (as teenagers, my boys called him the warden) was more Authoritarian with Authoritative tendencies. Even if you are not naturally a parent who fits into the Authoritative style of parenting, you can work towards that goal striving to be the best parent you can be to raise a child who grows up to be a happy, successful, responsible adult.

Your Job as Parents

You, as parents, are the rule setters and the enforcers of those rules. That is your job. When your child breaks the rules, there should be consequences for that behavior that are expected, not a surprise. When you enforce those consequences, you are just doing your job; it's what you are supposed to do. It's not being mean or a killjoy, you are just being a good parent. If your child breaks the rule, that is on them; you are just doing your job. If your child is obedient and abides by the rules, he or she should be praised and commended to reinforce that behavior. Deciding what rules to establish should be something that you both agree on and are willing to enforce. You should both be comfortable with the discipline plan.

So what rules or guidelines should you establish for your child? The rules should be easy to understand, age appropriate, and reasonable. For younger children, you may want to keep the list small and not too complicated. You may want to post the rules to make it easier to remember and make them clearly visible so there is no confusion. You don't want to be too strict, but you also don't want to be too lenient; it's a fine line that you will have to agree upon.

The purpose of teaching discipline to children is to help them to learn and grow in an environment that is nurturing, loving, and structured so that they will become healthy, well-adjusted adults who bring you joy and make you proud. If you discipline in anger and exasperate your children, you may not achieve the desired outcome. In Ephesians 6:4 (NLT), fathers are cautioned not to be too harsh with their children. It says,

> *Fathers, do not provoke your children to anger by the way you treat them. Rather, bring them up with the discipline and instruction that comes from the Lord.*

You want obedient children, but you also want them to know without a doubt that you love them. The rules are put in place for their safety and their benefit. Teach your children the Ten Commandments. Let them know what God expects of his children. In fact, that is a good place to start when establishing rules and guidelines. Having a well-defined plan makes it so much easier on you and your child – there is less room for power struggles because the rules are clear.

Your children need to know exactly what you expect from them. It gives them a sense of order and belonging (this is how we do it in my house); and it gives them a sense of stability. Before we eat, we wash our hands. Before we eat, we say grace. Before we go to bed, we brush our teeth. As soon as we get home from school, we do our homework. First, we do our chores, then we play. Whatever the rules are in your house, the anticipation of what comes next and the consistency you provide gives the child reassurance that you are in control, which in turn provides a sense of security and less anxiety.

It is a good idea to plainly communicate the reasons for the rules or boundaries. If children know the reason behind the rule, they may complain, but they are much more likely to comply. For instance, if you tell your child that you want them to be home by 8:00 pm, let them know why. Explain that it is important for their health to get the proper amount of sleep, and they need time to get ready for bed, and unwind a bit before bed. You can also add that it is safer for them to be in before dark, and it is your job to protect them.

Decision-Making Skills

Decision-making skills is one of the most critical life skills that you can teach your child. Giving them the choice of two or three options, gives them a sense of responsibility and promotes confidence and self-satisfaction. This is a critical life skill desperately needed when approaching adolescence. In this phase of life, children are exposed to so many more choices that are potentially harmful.

Prepare your children to face these choices with their eyes wide open. Let them know without a doubt that you expect them to say NO to drugs and drinking. Talk to them about the pitfalls of engaging in sexual relationships before marriage, the perils of cheating or stealing; share your viewpoint on abortion or any other subject that is important to you as parents. Explain your reasons, give examples of how going down that road could be devastating to their personal wellbeing and to you as a parent. Let them know you will love them no matter what, but take a firm stand on issues that are important to you.

Enforcing the Plan

Once you establish the rules, you need to be prepared to enforce them and do so consistently. If you let your children off the hook occasionally, they will expect you to do it again and again, and they will badger you until you give in. It is better not to open that door. Of course, if there are extenuating circumstances, and if it is warranted, you may want to cut them some slack, but be aware of the message you may be sending. Sharing the family rules with caregivers and grandparents is important for consistency. If everyone follows the same rules with the same consequences, it avoids confusion and sending mixed messages.

Establishing a plan for discipline and following through with it has several advantages besides the ones already mentioned. As your children learn the rules and successfully follow the rules, they will have more confidence in their ability to be responsible and will grow in maturity. It teaches them self-discipline and how to cope with uncomfortable feelings when the rules are inconvenient or contrary to what they want. They need an opportunity to experience feelings like sadness, anger, frustration, or boredom, and learn how to deal with them in a positive way.

When they don't always get their own way, that struggle helps them to develop patience and discourages that need for instant gratification. Guidelines for eating healthy foods, getting enough exercise, and limiting screen time teach them lasting good health habits. Rules also keep them safe and show them that you care – you control their environment, and it makes them feel more secure.

When (notice I said when, not if) your children rebel and cause significant heartache of disappointment, please don't play the blame game. Even if you build and establish a plan together and know the right thing to do, sometimes you will break your own rules – one of you will disagree with the other about who is too lenient or who is too strict. You are both human, and it will happen. If your child does break the rules and gets in more serious trouble, don't try to place blame on each other. You are a team; you are in this together. Stick together and you will be able to work it out more effectively and efficiently and still present a united front for your children.

Doing Chores

One last thing I wanted to mention about household rules and expectations. I am a firm believer in children being given chores to do on a regular basis. It takes effort on the parents' part to supervise chores, but studies show that children who do chores are more likely to become happy, independent, healthy adults. Working together as parents to allocate chores will eventually lighten your load, and you can teach your children valuable life skills in the process.

Assigning chores and expecting children to pitch in makes them feel like they are an active part of the family, contributing to the family, and giving them a sense of purpose. It teaches them responsibility, good habits, and necessary life skills, and teaches them to develop a stronger positive work ethic so that they can become self-sufficient adults who recognize that there is value and self-satisfaction in hard work and achievements.

When my children were young, we lived in a neighborhood with tons of kids, and very few of their friends had to do chores – or at least that is what they told me. But I insisted that in our house we do chores, and as soon as yours are done, you can go out with your friends. My children were certainly not perfect, but they did their chores, and they all have received praise for their good work ethics as adults. Please don't spoil your children. It only hurts them in the long run, and it can break your heart. Love your children, indulge them occasionally, but don't be fooled – lack of discipline and too much leniency are harmful to children.

Chapter 13 Study Question

If you had to describe yourself as a child, would you say that you were – an obedient good-natured child, a risk taker with an impulsive streak, a stubborn ornery rascal, or a troublemaker?

1. There are four basic parenting styles: Authoritative (best model), Authoritarian (harsh disciplinarian), Permissive (lenient), and Uninvolved (neglectful). Which style did your parents use? Which style best fits your approach? Is it a mixture of styles?

2. Do you find that you and your spouse often disagree about how to discipline the children? If so, what can you do to eliminate some of the conflict?

3. The Bible clearly states that children should honor their mother and father. How would you define your relationship with your parents? How did your parents treat their parents? Does this reflect what you are modeling to your children?

4. Have you established clear boundaries for your children and outlined the consequences of testing those boundaries? Why or why not? If you have not, is this something that you think would be beneficial to do?

5. Is it difficult for you to enforce the rules and make your children face the consequences of their actions? Do you struggle with defining the appropriate disciplinary measures? Share your ideas for appropriate disciplinary measures and strategies.

6. Do you think that you were well prepared or unprepared to make important decisions when you reached adolescence? What will you do to make sure that your children are well prepared for this stage of life when making good choices is so critical?

7. What is your viewpoint on children having chores to do on a regular basis? Do you believe it is a sound practice or do you think you shouldn't expect children to do chores? Why or why not?

CHAPTER 14

BLENDED FAMILIES

If you are part of a blended family, you are not alone. Blended families account for about 40% of the families in the United States, and the majority of us have had some experience with blended families as either a stepparent, a stepchild, a stepsibling, a step grandparent, or a close friend to someone fitting that description. The word blend, according to the dictionary, means to mingle intimately or unobtrusively; to combine into an integrated whole; to produce a harmonious effect. That is the ultimate desire for the blended family – to mingle intimately into an integrated whole to produce a harmonious effect. This is definitely possible, but it is not an easy task.

The divorce rate for first marriages is about 50%, but the divorce rate for second marriages with children is 67%, and it goes up to 73% for third marriages. Alarming statistics, indeed! Does that mean you are doomed to fail? Absolutely not! If you are determined to make this marriage last and your desire is to ensure that your blended family works, there are many resources to help you figure out the best approach. Unfortunately, less than half of the people entering into a blended family even read an article about this subject, and that may be a significant reason why so many marriages of blended families end in divorce. How do you avoid adding to these terrible statistics?

Preparation

Before you take the plunge, understand what you are facing. Forming a blended family will come with significant challenges that will take a great deal of time and patience. Just because you were married before and have children doesn't mean that you are prepared for this new life event. There are many complicated layers that make up a blended family – each family member has different ideas, different perspectives, and are in different phases of acceptance. Each individual family has different traditions and customs, different discipline styles, different values, and different priorities. There is so much blending to be done, so you need to be prepared.

Couples need to think through the challenges they are facing and talk about how to start working through the blending process before the marriage takes place. Premarital preparation can lower the risk of divorce by at least 30%. Once again, good communication is critical. Consider what your role as a parent/stepparent will be regarding discipline, boundaries, division of labor, expectations of time spent with your children and your spouse's children. Discuss your expectations for spending time with extended family. Talk about your long-term goals and financial plan. Understand that you may have to be flexible, willing to compromise and adjust your expectations.

If you can afford to do so, invest in a new home. If you move into one of your current homes, stuff will have to be moved and displaced to provide space for the newcomers, which will likely cause resentment and rivalry between family members. If you move into a new home, nothing has a previously designated space, no one has a prior claim to a particular space or room, and you are all starting with a clean blank space. There may still be squabbles about who gets which room, but no one's stuff is being displaced for someone else or being rearranged by someone else.

Choosing to move into a new home together also subtly conveys the message that we are dedicated to making this change permanent, we are investing in a safe secure environment for our new family, and there is no going back. We are now a blended family.

Priorities

Strong families are built on strong marriages. If there is no marriage, there is no family. As in all families, the marriage needs to have first priority to succeed. In a blended family, this can be so much more complicated because the previous single-parent families were an intact unit and settled in their own ways. Now every family member will have to adjust and adapt to being part of a new family unit. There is the tendency to want to put your children's needs above that of your spouse, but that will undermine the foundation of the new family unit.

Work together with your spouse to strengthen your bond of intimacy and commitment by consistently communicating, honoring each other's feelings, being respectful and compassionate as you face the challenges one by one. In Proverbs 18:19 (NLT), it says,

> *An offended friend is harder to win back than a fortified city.*
> *Arguments separate friends like a gate locked with bars.*

A marriage with a gate and locked bars between husband and wife is not ideal! Rather than fighting to do it your way, embrace what will be the new normal for your family, a blending of old ways and new ways that will give your family a face of its own. The children need to see you modeling a solid positive marriage relationship, and any deviation from that can be extremely detrimental to the stability of your family.

Stepparenting

You need to understand that each person in the new family unit will come with their individual perspectives. Children may not be motivated at first to embrace the new stepparent. They may feel that to do so would be disloyal to their other biological parent. They may be reluctant to get too close for fear that their new stepparent will end up leaving if the marriage doesn't last. They may just resent you because they are still hoping that their parents will get back together, or they may be simply mourning the loss of what used to be. You need to understand that they may not be ready to trust you yet, especially if they are older.

You must be prepared to take it slow because building a loving relationship between a stepparent and a stepchild requires tremendous patience, unwavering persistence, and a lot of love given unconditionally. You may be thinking that it will take a few weeks or months to win your stepchild over, but it will more likely take two to five years to establish that loving blended family that you are longing for. You will need to allow the stepchild to set the pace for building the relationship and not expect too much too soon.

When you try to discipline your stepchild, you will inevitably hear, "You are not my father!" or "You are not my mother!" In reply, I suggest that you agree. You are not his father (or mother), but you have been given authority by his father (or mother) to see that the family rules are followed. If the child has a problem with this authority, he or she should talk to the other parent about it. In the meantime, the rules are to be followed. This is part of the value of clearly stating the rules of the household before you are put in charge of your stepchildren.

You will need to not only pursue your stepchild with patience, but you will also need God's wisdom for guidance and direction. James 1:5 says,

> *If any of you lacks wisdom, you should ask God, who gives generously to all without finding fault, and it will be given to you.*

God sees and understands the bigger picture; you do not. You will not always be able to understand or relate to your stepchild's thinking or logic, but you need to respect his or her feelings. Seek godly wisdom to build that loving relationship. Be prepared to persistently show love even through rejection. You will likely face lots of it. In Romans 5:3-5 (NLT), Paul tells us,

> *We can rejoice, too, when we run into problems and trials, for we know that they help us develop endurance. And endurance develops strength of character, and character strengthens our confident hope of salvation. And this hope will not lead to disappointment. For we know how dearly God loves us, because he has given us the Holy Spirit to fill our hearts with his love.*

Stepparenting, or any parenting, is not for the faint of heart. You will face problems and trials, and this will help you to develop strength and endurance (which you will need), but take heart, because there is hope. You will eventually break down those barriers, even if it takes years, and the reward will be worth the hard work and diligent persistence you showed through the difficulties. God will honor your dedication and compassion for these children.

Here are a few suggestions for stepparenting that may help you to navigate the rough waters without capsizing the boat.

- ♥ Don't try to step in as the strict disciplinarian at first. Always present a united front but allow the biological parent to be the enforcer when possible. You have (hopefully) already established the rules and boundaries of the household. If you are left in charge of the children, the children should understand that they are expected to be obedient, respectful, and courteous. If not, there will be consequences.

♥ Don't try to be the replacement parent. Rather, work at building a new relationship between you that will be based on providing safety, security, stability, and support in a caring, nurturing environment. Find some common ground, a shared interest or a project that you can work on together to fortify your relationship.

♥ Make sharing family meals a priority. It provides a great opportunity to share thoughts and ideas and events that occurred during the day, encouraging good conversation. It helps to build tradition, a ritual they can count on, and it creates bonding within the family unit.

♥ Never denigrate the biological parent. It may be tempting to do so, especially if the parent is causing the child pain or disappointment, but it is simply not your place to slander or insult or belittle. The child needs you to be encouraging and supporting, not judgmental or self-righteous. Be sensitive to their feelings, be sympathetic and compassionate, but never condemning.

♥ Never show favoritism. If you both bring children into the blended family, be intentional and consistent with all the children in the household, always disciplining and showing affection without favoritism. Showing favoritism may be the most destructive thing you can do in a blended family – it will cause a rift between you and your spouse, and it will hinder your efforts to build that relationship with your stepchildren causing anger, bitterness, and resentment to enter in.

♥ Do spend one-on-one time with each child, your own children and your stepchildren, and encourage your spouse to do the same. The goal is to build a loving, solid relationship with each individual person within the family, and giving your precious time to that endeavor will be most beneficial. Appreciate each child's special qualities and talents. Your biological children need to have you all to themselves occasionally, but you need to do the same for your stepchildren.

♥ Find out what your stepchild's love language is (refer to Chapter 6) and use that information to help your relationship to be strengthened and grow.

♥ Do spend one-on-one time with your spouse and have a date night at least once a month. Remember, your marriage is the foundation of your family and it needs to be a priority for the family to succeed and flourish. Nurture your relationship with each other, and guard it carefully.

♥ Be intentional about blending the family traditions of the old families, as well as establishing new traditions and rituals. This goes a long way in creating a sense of unity and harmony. Take family vacations together, create new memories, and do things together as a family on a regular basis – hiking, biking, picnicking, visiting family, movie nights, game nights – be creative and make it fun.

♥ Integrating into a new extended family can be complicated as well. Grandparents, just like parents, need to be careful about showing favoritism. There needs to be an equitable division of time, attention, and money spent on gifts. This can provide a stabilizing influence for the entire family if all members are accepted and loved by grandparents, aunts, uncles, cousins, etc. A note to step grandparents, again just like the stepparent, you need to take things slowly, giving the child time to adjust to the new family. Don't expect the step grandchildren to instantly fall in love with you. Allow them to set the pace for the relationship, gently encouraging them with love and understanding.

♥ Adult children may have objections to the marriage and blending of families. They may have valid concerns about the marriage, possibly even seeing red flags regarding the person you plan to marry that you don't see. They may be concerned that the inheritance they were expecting to come to them will be diverted to the new spouse. They may feel that you are being disloyal to your former spouse or that they are being disloyal by accepting the new spouse. Talk with each of your children privately. Allow them to voice their concerns with an open mind. You need to validate their feelings, letting them know that you understand what they are saying, but . . . Then in all fairness, they should allow you to voice your thoughts and feelings. Help them to understand why this person is so important to you. Ask them to look at the situation from your perspective. Communication can make all the difference between a strained uncomfortable relationship and open acceptance. They don't have to love your wife and her family, they just need to respect your choices, honor your feelings, treat your spouse and the other family members with kindness and respect, being courteous and polite. You may need to give your children some time and the space they need to make the adjustment to your new lifestyle, but work at keeping those lines of communication open.

♥ When you and your spouse have disagreements, always argue in private. Your children need to see you both exhibiting a safe secure marital foundation for the sake of their stability. Be aware that your children's eyes are constantly watching how you interact with each other, especially in the early stages. If you have a disagreement in front of your children, you may see it as nothing, but it may cause your child or children undue anxiety and stress.

♥ If you and your family are struggling to make things work, there are so many resources available to parents of blended families. One of the best books that I would highly recommend is *Building Love Together in Blended Families* by Gary Chapman and Ron Deal. The book goes into much more detail about how to create a safe and loving environment amidst the complicated dynamics and trust issues in a blended family.[7] Gary Chapman also talks about the five love languages that people respond to in a relationship. He says relationships grow better and stronger when we understand each other better in terms of how we receive and give love differently.

♥ If you are still struggling, don't hesitate to seek out other couples who have successfully blended their families. Their personal perspectives may offer invaluable insight that helps provide some clarity for your situation, and it always helps to know you are not alone in your struggles and that you have someone you can confide in who understands.

♥ If you have more specific and complex issues that need to be addressed, seek out professional help, preferably from a Christian counselor who will understand and support a biblical approach to parenting. If you are having difficulty finding a Christian counselor, ask your pastor for a referral.

Blending two families together and providing a safe, secure, and loving environment is a very precious gift to give to your children. Those in a blended family versus a single parent home offer more stability, both emotionally and financially, and once successfully blended, your children will have the benefit of more family to claim as their own.

Research has found that having siblings increases your overall happiness and health. When you have siblings who love you, they can provide support, protection, and encouragement as you face obstacles in life together. They can inspire you with motivation and inspiration to be your best self, even long after your parents are gone. Personally speaking, I am so very thankful for my siblings and their families because they enrich my life beyond measure.

Blending families is hard work. It can be frustrating, even infuriating, but if you are loving, patient, and persistent, the rewards will be worth more than you can imagine. It is a labor of love, unconditional love that puts the other person's needs above their own. As they say, nothing worth having ever comes easy. Invest yourself in your family – your time, your talents, your money, and your heart – and you will enjoy the rich rewards for a lifetime.

Chapter 14 Making It Personal

What is the most memorable moment you had as a blended family?

1. What preparation did you make before you blended your families? Do you wish you would have done more preparation? What is one thing you wish you prepared for and didn't?

2. As a blended family, you are strongly encouraged to give your marriage relationship first priority to preserve the family unit. Do you agree with this principle? Is this difficult for you? Why or why not?

3. Would you say that your transition into being a blended family was easier than you thought, what you expected, or harder than you thought it would be? Explain.

4. Describe your relationships with your stepchildren and your strategy for building and strengthening that relationship. Have you asked God for wisdom and guidance to get you through the challenges?

5. What is the biggest challenge you have faced as a blended family?

6. What is the most rewarding moment you have experienced as a blended family?

7. Have you sought out other couples who have successfully blended their families? Did you find this to be beneficial? Why or why not?

8. What advice would you give to a couple planning to marry and blend their families?

CHAPTER 15
RENEW AND REFRESH

Renew means to make new or restore; refresh means to revitalize. Everything needs to be renewed and refreshed occasionally, especially marriages. Following the same routines day in and day out, our relationships can grow stale and stagnant, and they need some fresh attention to bring back the energy and luster, to restore the strength and beauty of the loving relationship.

Is it worth pouring the time and effort it takes to renew and refresh the relationship? Absolutely, in fact, there is great value in maintaining a marriage relationship. What are the benefits of staying married? Well, according to the current research, the studies consistently show that men and women are:

♥ More likely to live longer

♥ More likely to be physically healthier

♥ More likely to be mentally healthier

♥ More likely to be happier

♥ Recover from illness quicker and more successfully

♥ Generally, take better care of themselves and avoid risky behavior[9]

These are excellent reasons to motivate you to place a high priority on your renewing and refreshing your marriage relationship.

But why do marriage relationships tend to grow stale and dull after a period of time? I think that we just get so caught up in our busy lives, putting one foot in front of the other, dealing with a multitude of stressors, that we don't even realize it is happening until one day you wake up and realize that this is no fun anymore. What can you do about it? You can just resign yourself to a dull, monotonous relationship, or you can take the initiative to renew and refresh your marriage. With some concentrated effort and determination, you can restore it to its full power and potential. Don't wait until your marriage is struggling, do it now.

Perhaps you recognize that your relationship is starting to lose its spark, and you don't know where to start. Well, I have a few suggestions that can help you to rejuvenate yourself and your marriage relationship. Let's explore each one and choose the ones best suited to your relationship.

Reclaim the Romance

Romance is one of the core desires of our hearts, the stuff of dreams and fantasies. We women dream of the Prince Charming who will sweep us off our feet, lavish us with roses, whisper sweet nothings in our ears, and offer us that happily ever after. Men are most often the ones charged with being responsible for providing the romance, but men need romance in their lives every bit as much as women do. We all long for that sweet relationship filled with love, excitement, connection, and affection.

The more romance you have in your relationship, the more intimacy you share. A natural consequence of that deeper intimacy is a more passionate relationship. So how do you revive the romance? You need to be intentional. You need to have a plan. It doesn't have to be a huge, grand gesture like buying your wife a car and putting a bow on it. It is the small things that say "I love you" that we hold dear to our hearts.

One year for our anniversary, my husband bought me three cards. He put one on the kitchen counter propped up against the coffee pot. He put a second one in my car along with my favorite candy bar that I found as I was going to work. The third one was waiting for me when I got home along with two little stuffed bears hugging a heart that said, "Happy Anniversary." He probably spent less than $20, but I thought that it was so romantic. That was over 10 years ago, and I still have the little stuffed bears in my office, and every time I see them, I smile with fond remembrance.

Always take advantage of Valentine's Day and Anniversaries to let your loved one know that you care, that you think he or she is special enough to celebrate. You don't have to stress over what to buy but make it heartfelt. Back in our early days when money was tight, I gave my husband coupons for things like a "free" neck massage, a foot rub, his favorite dinner, a truck wash – things I knew he would appreciate that weren't on my normal list of routine jobs. Other times my husband brought me a single rose; somehow, I think that is more romantic than a dozen long-stemmed roses. It doesn't have to be grand or fancy, it just has to come from the heart. I know how much my husband hates to shop, so if he goes out and buys me a gift, no matter what it is, I appreciate the gesture so much.

Date Night

Do you make time to go out on regular dates? Well, in my opinion, you should. You both need to connect one-on-one on a consistent basis to maintain that personal bond with one another. When you are out together, make each other a priority and give your undivided attention – that means no texting or phone calls (except emergencies, of course).

Make date night fun. You might want to take turns deciding what to do for the evening. Just going out to dinner is great, but a little mundane. Take an afternoon and go for a bike ride or a hike in the woods. Commit to doing a project together. Volunteer at the local animal shelter or do ministry together. Try something new like a dance class or a cooking class to spice things up (ha-ha – get it? spice things up). Go out with other couples who are fun to be around that you can laugh with and have a good time.

Be spontaneous. Surprise each other. One weekend, I kidnapped my husband. I secretly arranged for a weekend getaway, and he had no idea. I had packed our bags and hid them in the trunk. He thought we were going to visit his sister (which was in the same direction), but when he got to the turnoff to go to her house, I confessed what was up. I gave him directions as we drove. He didn't know our destination until we arrived. It was fun, spontaneous, and turned out to be quite a memorable weekend.

Another final note about date night – be affectionate. Hold hands, put your arm around her shoulder, touch his cheek, look into each other's eyes. Share a real kiss, not just a quick peck, but a real kiss. You are in this together, you both deserve a rich, rewarding relationship. Sure, it takes time and effort and planning, but the payoff is priceless. Enjoy each other.

Communication Counts

♥ Compliments

Yes, we are going to talk about communication one more time – that is how important it is! Let's start with compliments. They are absolutely free; they cost you nothing and offer rich rewards. Everyone likes to receive compliments, especially if they know the words are sincere. How awesome to receive praise for something you did or said, or on how you look. Kind words can relieve tension, they can bring healing and restoration where there's sadness. They can put a smile on someone's face and brighten the day. When you offer compliments, the recipient feels a greater satisfaction with the relationship and more connected to you. Don't miss out on these opportunities to connect.

Use your words to compliment your spouse often, at least once a day. Look for chances to encourage your spouse, to be supportive, to make your spouse feel loved. You will be surprised how just one compliment can positively impact the dynamic of your conversation when you are sincere. This can be true of any relationship – compliment a coworker on a job well done, compliment the waitress on the quality of service, compliment the chef for a great meal, compliment the soccer coach on his dedication, compliment your son on his good manners, compliment your daughter on her great report card – the list can go on and on.

In this age of so much negativity, be the positive energy in someone's day – offer compliments and encouragement and it will brighten your day as well. And when someone pays you a compliment, don't contradict them or look embarrassed, smile and say, "Thank You!"

♥ Share Your Dreams

A great topic of conversation for developing a deeper connection with your spouse is to share your hopes and dreams and desires. It requires a certain level of trust to share the secrets of your heart with someone else, but a healthier level of trust leads to more profound level of intimacy. What is your dream, your vision for your marriage? Does the reality live up to the dream? If not, why not? You may want to talk about how you can get there. Be open-minded, embrace the possibilities, and share.

If your spouse shares a dream or desire, be willing to accept and encourage your partner, even if you don't understand it. Change and personal growth are good for a relationship, providing stimulation and avoiding that staleness of stagnation. Be supportive and encourage your spouse to achieve his or her dream – it can only strengthen your relationship.

I had always wanted to go to college, but I married young and that never happened. I was always too busy being a wife and a mom. When my youngest child graduated high school and was getting ready to leave for college, I had this strong desire to go back to school and get my degree. I was in my early 50's at that point, and it didn't make sense to my husband or my kids. They all thought I was going through an empty nest crisis or a mid-life crisis; they thought it was a crazy idea.

But I was serious about pursuing my degree, and I really wanted to do it, but if my husband discouraged me, I probably would have sadly given up on my dream. It would be a bit of a hardship financially, so I was hesitant about spending the money. My husband didn't discourage me. He said that if this is something you really want to do, I think you should go for it. I can't even begin to tell you how much his support and encouragement meant to me! If you discourage your spouse, it could open the door for resentment to come in because of unrealized dreams. Help your spouse to realize his or her dreams, and you can celebrate the successes together.

♥ Tough Conversations

Is there tension in your relationship making it difficult for you to feel refreshed and renewed? There will undoubtedly be tough conversations occasionally that you will have to navigate through as you do life together. If you need to clear the air, don't put off having the tough conversations because that will only increase tension and eat away at your relationship. Even though it may be uncomfortable, it is always best to just do it.

Here are some suggestions for talking it through with the best possible outcome. If there is a topic you need to discuss where you have differing viewpoints, ask your spouse to share his or her opinion first. Listen empathetically with an open mind; do not criticize or interrupt. You will have your turn. You don't have to offer advice or "fix it," you just have to listen attentively.

Then, when you are sure that your spouse has had ample opportunity to share, respectfully and tactfully share your opinion. Honesty inspires trust, so be truthful and straightforward. Once you are finished, ask for feedback. Talk about both perspectives respectfully, and brainstorm solutions. Be willing to compromise and be flexible. You are in this together, so you want to come to an agreement that is good and acceptable for both of you so that you can both feel refreshed and renewed.

"Me" Time

When you are stressed and overwhelmed with so much to do and so little time, self-care is usually the first thing we eliminate, especially women. We feel guilty taking time for ourselves because there is so little spare time. Some of us don't like to admit we need time for renewal and refreshment. We can do it all; we are superheroes! NO, you are NOT! You cannot be fully effective and function at your best if you don't recharge your batteries at least once a week.

You may ask how can I take time out for myself when there are not enough hours in the day now? Finding the time will be worth the payoff. You don't have to take a whole day, even if it is just two hours once a week, it will help to rejuvenate you, especially if it is a regular weekly event, you can look forward to.

The first step is to admit that you NEED time for yourself – it's not a frivolous waste of time, it is for the benefit of your health and well-being so that you can function at your best. Make it a priority. Talk with your spouse about how you can each carve out some time to get a break. Not only for you, but for your spouse as well. You can encourage each other to take your "me" time.

So how do you carve time out from such a hectic schedule? You accept some help and support. When my family and I were going through a really tough time, friends and family members would ask me what they can do to help, and I would say "there is really nothing, I've got it covered." I was lying; it was a pride issue. It is so much easier to give help than to receive it. I didn't know how to ask for help, and when I did realize I needed help, I was embarrassed and afraid they would say no. That may sound silly, but it was true. I realize now that my friends really wanted to help, and I wouldn't let them in, so they felt useless. If you are in the same position, here is a tip for enlisting support.

Make a list of things that could help you out so that you are ready when someone offers or says, "I wish I could help" (picking your son up from soccer practice, going with you to a stressful doctor appointment, watching the kids for an hour so you can take a walk or go to the grocery store or run errands, babysitting for a date night or to go to a support group). Sure, you could do some of those things with the kids, but we all need the occasional break!

What are some things you can do to relax and unwind?

- Enjoy nature. Take a walk.
- Jog or exercise. Dance it out.
- Play basketball or racquetball.
- Have lunch with a friend.
- Do conscious breathing. Meditate.
- Get a massage or a mani/pedi.
- Take a power nap. Take a bubble bath.
- Write in a journal.
- Take time out for daily devotions to feed your spiritual needs.

Taking care of spiritual needs is so important to your emotional wellbeing! Isaiah 40.31 says,

"but those who hope in the Lord will renew their strength. They will soar on wings like eagles; they will run and not grow weary, they will walk and not be faint."

I would hear that verse, and I would say, "God, I need to renew my strength. I want to be able to run and not grow weary" because I felt weary all the time. I didn't make time to recharge my batteries often enough. I pray that you do not make the same mistake.

Whatever you chose to do during your "me" time, do something consistently. Remember, it needs to be a priority for both of you. You are in this together, so support each other and encourage each other to refresh and renew – you owe it to yourself and to your family.

Intimacy and Sex

The main point of oiling a piece of machinery is to reduce the friction between the moving parts. As the oil lubricates the moving parts, it helps to reduce the wear and tear on the machine, it prevents machine downtime, it controls machine temperatures, and it serves to block any contamination from getting into the machine, acting like a filter. It may sound odd to compare an intimate sexual relationship to a well-oiled machine but humor me for a moment and consider the similarities.

A healthy sexual relationship is like the oil that keeps the machine (marriage) running effectively and smoothly. It helps to reduce the wear and tear on the pieces (husband and wife), because they are in tune with each other, in love, and more willing to overlook each other's faults. The oil (sex) keeps the temperatures (tempers) from getting out of control because the moving parts (husband and wife) are in balance with each other. Outside sources of contaminants are filtered out because the relationship is strong enough to filter out the gunk that could clog up the machine (marriage).

When the sexual relationship is not working, the oil dries up and the moving parts (husband and wife) experience increased friction. All those little irritants and contaminants threaten the smooth operation of the machine (marriage), and you may have unwanted downtime due to the machine (marriage) not running smoothly. A healthy sexual relationship is like the oil that keeps the marriage running smoothly.

Every marriage goes through difficult challenges and rough spots over the years that can wreak havoc with the passion in your marriage. It is unrealistic to think this won't happen at some point in your marriage, or even at several points. The important thing to remember is to not let this rough spot become the new normal and destroy your intimate relationship. Don't settle for less. Marriage was designed to be an institution with a close intimate relationship that is both fulfilling and richly satisfying.

The intimate passionate kiss that you share reduces stress hormones and lowers blood pressure. The power of touch is like the secret weapon in a successful personal relationship. Hugs from a loved one give us that warm fuzzy feeling. The power of touch can be exhilarating and telling.

Laura Guerrero, coauthor of Close Encounters: Communication in Relationships, states: "While couples who are satisfied with each other do tend to touch more, the true indicator of a healthy long-term bond is not how often your partner touches you but how often he or she touches you in response to your touch. The stronger the reciprocity, the more likely someone is to report emotional intimacy and satisfaction with the relationship. As with many things in relationships, satisfaction is as much about what we do for our partner as about what we're getting."[6.]

The intimate relationship works best if it is balanced, reciprocal, fun, spontaneous, and flirty. The next time you get in an argument and tensions are high, try "hugging it out." It will calm you both and the power of touch is amazingly healing. Your spouse may think you are a little crazy if you suggest "hugging it out," but it is tough to argue when you are hugging, and it may just lead to a make up session.

A Gift for Your Marriage

A beautiful gift to give yourselves is to invest in your marriage by attending a Christian Marriage Retreat. Whether your marriage is good or troubled, your marriage will be strengthened, enriched, and renewed. At these interactive retreats, you are typically offered intensive counseling by trained professional therapists who are there to help you restore, heal, and transform your relationship, taking it to a new level. You will gain insight into how to revitalize your relationship and leave with renewed love and intimacy.

To search for a retreat that works best for you, I would suggest Googling "Christian Marriage Retreats" and see what is available. My husband and I attended one about 10 years ago, and I would highly recommend it. All the couples we attended with said their relationships benefited greatly from the experience. If you are still in doubt, read the reviews. I know you won't be disappointed. Treat yourselves to a marriage enriching weekend. You deserve it!

Chapter 15 Making It Personal

When was the last time you took a day for renewal and refreshment?

1. When was the last time you did something special (out of the ordinary) for your spouse? Are you overdue for some romantic gesture?

2. When was your last date night? What did you do together? Was it a fun evening or just so-so? What could you do to liven things up?

3. Do you find it easier to give or receive compliments? Do you compliment your spouse often? Why or why not?

4. Have you openly shared your dreams and goals with your spouse? How did he or she respond?

5. Have you asked your spouse what his or her dreams and goals are? If so, how can you be an encouragement or offer support?

6. What do you like to do to recharge? How can you make this a priority and be consistent?

7. What kind of gunk gas gotten into your machine to plug it up? What can you do to get the machine running efficiently once again?

8. Have you ever attended a marriage retreat? If so, did you benefit from the experience? If not, why not?

CHAPTER 16

THE EMPTY NEST

You both worked hard to provide a good home for your children, and it was a labor of love. You invested much of your time, effort, and money into raising your children together. The crazy rollercoaster ride is over. They are now independent adults, living on their own, and making their own way in the world. That phase of your life is over. Now it's your turn to focus your energy on each other. It sounds simple, idyllic, and refreshing, right? But what if it is not what you expected?

You have both poured your lives into your children – going to soccer games, hockey games, football games, music lessons, recitals, plays, school events – now that is over. You suddenly find this huge void between you and this person you have partnered with all these years. The kids filled the gap, served as a buffer of sorts, and now there is a big empty hole. This strange emptiness is uncomfortable, awkward, maybe even scary. Now what? The transition into this new phase of life is not always smooth.

Change is hard and moving from one phase of life to another can be confusing and complicated. You are dealing with the loss of what you left behind and going forward into uncharted territory. Since the kids are gone, you and your spouse may struggle to find things to talk about, your common thread vaporized. Can your relationship survive? Absolutely, but it will take time and effort to rebuild and reconnect.

You now have more time on your hands, and some couples use this time to find fault with their spouse – focusing on disappointments or expectations that were not met or focusing on problems in the marriage that were never resolved and have suddenly become a major issue. In fact, you may both be focusing on the negative aspects of your relationship. You probably have both been a disappointment to each other at some point in your marriage. Matthew 7:3 says,

> *Why do you look at the speck of sawdust in your brother's eye and pay no attention to the plank in your own eye?*

No one is perfect, not even you! Instead of focusing on the negative aspects, focus on how to fix those issues and work towards fulfilling those unmet expectations together. If you need some advice, guidance, or direction, seek out another Christian couple who have been married for a number of years and have stayed the course in spite of life's ups and downs. They may be able to share some of their invaluable hard-earned wisdom for making it work.

Sometimes, if the problems are very personal and difficult to discuss with others, you may want to seek help from a Christian marriage counselor to bridge the gap, and it may help to make the transition easier, especially if there are unresolved problems in the marriage.

My husband and I had an unresolved issue in our marriage that ended up taking center stage when we encountered the empty nest. To me, it seemed overwhelming and insurmountable, a problem with no resolution and no clear answers. But with the help of a Christian counselor and considerable time praying about it, the problem resolved itself, much to my surprise. Never underestimate the power of prayer! As you seek to move through this new stage of life, persistently pray for guidance and direction, and I promise that God will not disappoint you. He won't necessarily make it easy for you, but he will get you through it one day at a time.

Let's face it, you are both adjusting to your new roles in life. You may even be facing retirement at this point. You are in the process of redefining your purpose, your mission, and your goals. It is time to start living the life that you postponed for so many years and think about what YOU want to do next. Both of you are making this transition, so do it together!

How do you start? By reconnecting on a more personal level. Here it is again! Communication is key. Good communication can draw you together; lack of communication can pull you apart and lead to isolation and loneliness, making you feel like you are struggling all by yourself. There is a real danger here of an emotional divorce – refusing to let your spouse in, focusing inward, putting up barriers, isolating and distancing yourself from your spouse is risky. This leaves you very vulnerable to assaults on your marriage.

Remember, the devil's desire is to steal, kill, and destroy (John 10:10), and you don't want to give him a way in to sabotage your marriage. He would like nothing better than to destroy your marriage and wreak havoc on both of you and your family. You have invested many years of your life to this relationship. Protect your investment. Fight for it. Guard your marriage diligently. Focus on reconnecting, rebuilding, and restoring your relationship to its former glory. You don't want your marriage to just survive, you want it to thrive. Strive to rekindle the romance and passion. Don't settle for less, you both deserve more. Start by reconnecting and rebuilding.

Reconnect and Rebuild

Again, it starts with good communication. Reconnecting with your spouse means opening the door to a fresh renewal of your friendship, reestablishing a camaraderie between you. Turn off the TV, your computer, and your cellphone and devote time to each other. Talk about what you are feeling and thinking during this transitioning phase. Offer each other support and reassurance through the redefinition process, as you seek to redefine your purpose, your mission, and your goals. Discuss the possibilities, consider the options, and encourage your spouse to follow the dream that has been on hold for so many years or to pursue a new dream.

You are never too old to dream, to try new things. If you are in your 60s, I would not recommend taking up rock climbing, but find something new that excites you and invigorates you. Psalm 92:12-15 (emphasis added) inspires us to keep going. It says,

> *The righteous will flourish like a palm tree,*
> *they will grow like a cedar of Lebanon;*
> *planted in the house of the Lord,*
> *they will **flourish** in the courts of our God.*
> *They will still **bear fruit in old age**,*
> *they will **stay fresh and green**,*
> *proclaiming, "The Lord is upright;*
> *he is my Rock, and there is no wickedness in him."*

You will still bear fruit in old age and stay fresh and green and flourish if you don't give up on yourself or each other. As you discuss the possibilities for your future together, keep an open mind and explore all options. Think big, be willing to take a risk, be adventurous. This is not the time to criticize or find fault with an idea. Be willing to talk it through and find out why the idea is important to your spouse. If you shut down an idea without exploring the possibility first, it will shut down communication and erect barriers between you, and that is something you want to avoid.

You may each want to pick something new to try – a cooking class, dance lessons, gardening, a daily walk or another type of exercise, a new fellowship group, or volunteer together. Be willing to embrace new ideas, new routines, new hobbies, and lifestyle changes. Be flexible and willing to compromise. You both still have a lot of living to do – make it fun and exciting together.

Now is a great time to resume regular date nights if you have let that slide. Enjoy an intimate evening out with just the two of you or indulge in a romantic getaway to bring back the romance and rekindle that passion you had for each other 20 years ago. Talk about the early days and reminisce about the fun times you shared. Make it extra special with a surprise little gift or a heartfelt toast to your new phase of life. Be creative. Be intentional. Be enthusiastic. Be joyful. Be the person that your spouse fell in love with.

Now if you're like me, you don't look quite the same as you did at 25, and maybe, like me, you were a little bit slimmer and a little less wrinkly, but your spouse is probably in the same boat. You are both still the same person inside, the person your spouse chose to love, honor, and cherish. You are the one who was chosen, build on that, invest in that, hold onto that.

Another way to add some zest into your marriage is to revitalize your social calendar – ask another couple to join you for dinner, reach out to old friends or make new friends by joining a book club or a golf league, or volunteer for a new ministry together. Go out dancing, go see a play, go to the beach, go hiking, have fun. Take every opportunity to celebrate the milestones in your life – the anniversaries, birthdays, events, new beginnings.

My husband and I are both retired. He has his hobby (restoring old cars), and I have my hobbies (writing and reading and gardening). I have no interest in old cars, but I go to car shows with him occasionally and enjoy going for rides in his old muscle cars. He helps me with the heavier gardening chores, and he encourages me to continue my writing. We have our own hobbies but making sure they overlap at times helps to keep our interests connected to each other.

We enjoy travelling together (to be honest I enjoy that more than he does). We have a large group of friends that we go out to dinner with or gather in each other's homes several times a month. We also make it a point to connect every morning over a cup of coffee before breakfast, and every afternoon at 3:00 pm, we have a "beer break." He enjoys a beer and I have a glass of wine either sitting in front of the gas fireplace or on the porch when the weather is nice. We sit side-by-side and talk and sometimes cuddle. It's our way of staying connected throughout the day and being intentional about spending quality time together.

Find a way to connect regularly that fits your lifestyle and preferences. I have friends who started biking; another couple is making plans to visit every one of our fifty states; another couple decided to open a bed and breakfast, and yet another couple started fly fishing. The possibilities are endless. Discover what your next adventure will be and start to enjoy each other's company again.

If the transition from the empty nest is more difficult than you can manage on your own, I would strongly encourage you to seek professional help through a Christian marriage counselor. Ask your pastor for a recommendation if you are not sure where to begin. A counselor can help you to rediscover the heart of your marriage commitment and build a lasting relationship that is better than ever before.

Whatever you decide to do, be proactive and find ways to infuse your relationship with new vitality. Don't settle for a lifeless loveless marriage. You both deserve to be happy in your relationship. This is your time, don't waste it! You are in this together, so work together to reconnect, rebuild, and restore your marriage. We all long for a healthy vibrant marriage, so make the most of your relationship. Enjoy!

Chapter 16 Making It Personal

Does the thought of an empty nest fill you will delight, sadness, confusion, or fear?

1. I have come to believe that there basically are two kinds of people: those who embrace change looking forward to the next new adventure (rare) or those who don't like change and are very uncomfortable with the thought of what comes next (more common). Which category do you fit into? Explain your answer. How do you think the empty nest will impact your life?

2. Moving into the empty nest phase usually means you have more time on your hands, and sometimes spouses use that extra time to think critically about their partner. Do you struggle with being too critical at times? Do you tend to focus on the negative characteristics? Do you feel your spouse is critical of you? If so, what can you do to encourage a more positive focus?

3. After learning about skillful communication, how would you rate your communication skills when speaking with your spouse on a scale of 1 to 10 (1 being poor and 10 being excellent)? How would you rate your spouse's communication skills?

4. What could you do to improve communication between you to be more constructive, more effective, and more considerate of each other?

5. Have you thought about what you will do to fill your empty nest? Do you have a dream that you have put on hold or something that you always longed to do? Is there something that you could do as a couple that would energize your relationship?

6. Would you consider yourself to be a hopeless romantic or not so much? When was the last time you attempted to inject some romance into your relationship? Are you way overdue to invest in some romantic gesture? How would your spouse answer those questions?

7. What could you do this week to show your partner that he or she is loved? Talk about ways you can inspire each other to be more romantic and strengthen your relationship.

REFERENCES

1. Stanton, Glenn (2011) <u>Divorce Rate in the Church – As High as the World? - Focus on the Family</u>

2. UWA (2019) The Science of Emotion: Exploring the Basics of Emotional Psychology

   Psychology and Counseling News <u>The Science of Emotion: Exploring the Basics of Emotional Psychology | UWA Online</u>

3. Collins (2021) *Emotional Baggage Definition and Meaning* <u>Emotional baggage definition and meaning | Collins English Dictionary (collinsdictionary.com)</u>

4. Colic reference: <u>www.mayoclinic.org/diseases-conditions/colic/symptoms-causes/syc-20371074</u>

5. Chapman, G. (2015) *The 5 Love Languages: The Secret to Love that Lasts, New Edition.* Chicago: Northfield Publishing.

6. <u>The Impact of Divorce on Young Children and Adolescents | Psychology Today</u> December 19, 2011

7. Chapman, G. and Deal, R. (2020) *Building Love Together in Blended Families.* Chicago: Northfield Publishing.

8. Guerrero, Laura (2021) *Close Encounters: Communication in Relationships.* Thousand Oaks, CA: SAGE

9. Stanton, Glenn (2012) <u>The Health Benefits of Marriage - Focus on the Family</u>

ABOUT THE AUTHOR

Janis Lipinski is a published Author, Inspirational Speaker, and Bible Teacher who thrives on sharing encouraging, uplifting messages with her audience. She is the author of two books: *A Story of Joy,* and her latest book, *In This Together, Discover Secrets for Strengthening Your Marriage.*

Janis retired from her career as a geriatric care consultant, a career that was born out of her desire to help others who were struggling to find the best care for their loved ones. She has a Human Services B.S. Degree from Geneva College, and holds certifications in Gerontology, Professional Care Management, and Therapeutic Crisis Intervention. She is an active member of Crossroads Church in Pittsburgh and has been a follower of Jesus for over forty years. Janis has been married to her husband Denny for forty-nine years, and they live in McDonald, Pennsylvania. Their three children are grown now with families of their own, and they feel so blessed to have three wonderful grandchildren. Janis enjoys gardening, reading, writing, and traveling.

If you found this book helpful, consider leaving a review.
It helps others find this book.

OTHER BOOKS WRITTEN BY JANIS LIPINSKI

A Story of Joy (Elm Hill, 2019)

Purchase available at janislipinski.com

Made in the USA
Monee, IL
11 January 2022